Bf 110 G-2/U1 night fighter
equipped with two 300-litre drop-
tanks. (See pages 104–13.)

FIGHTERS OF THE LUFTWAFFE

Joachim Dressel and Manfred Greihl

TRANSLATED BY M. J. SHIELDS, FIInfSc, MITL

ARMS AND
ARMOUR

Arms and Armour Press
A CASSELL IMPRINT
Villiers House, 41-47 Strand, London WC2N 5JE.

Distributed in the USA by Sterling Publishing Co. Inc.,
387 Park Avenue South, New York, NY 10016-8810.

Distributed in Australia by Capricorn Link (Australia) Pty.
Ltd, P.O. Box 665, Lane Cove, New South Wales 2066.

British Library Cataloguing-in-Publication Data: a
catalogue record for this book is available from the British
Library

ISBN 1-85409-139-5

Designed and edited by DAG Publications Ltd.
Designed by David Gibbons; edited by Michael Boxall;
layout by Anthony A. Evans; camerawork by M&E
Reproductions, North Fambridge, Essex; printed and
bound in Great Britain by The Bath Press, Avon.

Contents

Notes

As German and British or American Air Force organization and ranks do not correspond exactly, the German names have been retained in the text.

Organization

During the Second World War a Luftwaffe Geschwader was roughly equivalent to an RAF Group, a Gruppe to a Wing, and a Staffel to a Squadron.

Depending on their function, these could carry a prefix such as Erprobungs- (Test-), Fernaufklärungs- (Long-Range Reconnaissance), Jagd- (Day Fighter), Kampf- (Bomber), Nachtjagd (Night-Fighter), Nahaufklärungs- (Close-Reconnaissance), Schlacht- (Close-Support), Zerstörer- (Heavy-Fighter), etc. Geschwader were referred to by abbreviations (e.g., JG - Jagdgeschwader), Gruppe within a Geschwader by a Roman numeral (e.g., I./JG 4), and Staffel by Arabic numerals (e.g., 1./JG 4).

Ranks

Luftwaffe	*RAF*	*USAAF*
Generalfeldmarschall	Marshal of the RAF	General (5-star)
Generaloberst	Air Chief Marshal	General (4-star)
General der Flieger	Air Marshal	Lieutenant General
Generalleutnant	Air Vice-Marshal	Major General
Oberst	Group Captain	Colonel
Oberstleutnant	Wing Commander	Lieutenant Colonel
Major	Squadron Leader	Major
Hauptmann	Flight Lieutenant	Captain
Oberleutnant	Flying Officer	First Lieutenant
Leutnant	Pilot Officer	Second Lieutenant

Abbreviations

Some abbreviations are used in text. Many have no special meaning, but the more important ones other than those indicated above are:

DLV	Deutscher Luftsportverband	German Air Sport League
E-Stelle	Erprobungstelle	Test Establishment
GdJ	General der Jagdflieger	General of Fighters
Jabo	Jadgbomber	Fighter-Bomber
KdE	Kommando der Erprobungstellen	Test Establishment Command
MG	Maschinengewehr	Machine-gun
MK	Motorkanone	Cannon
OKL	Oberkommando der Luftwaffe	Air Force High Command
RLM	Reichsluftfahrtsministerium	Air Ministry
RMfRuK	Reichsministerium für Rüstungskraft	War Supply Ministry
Stuka	Sturzkampfflugzeug	Dive-bomber
TLR	Technischer Luftrüstung	Technical Air Armament

Introduction

In the early 1920s a small body of officers in the 100,000-man German Reichswehr was secretly involved in building a new Luftwaffe. Felmy, Kesselring, Sperrle, Stumpf and Wever were the men of these early days. Between 1928 and 1931 many officers of the Reichswehr were trained for the future Luftwaffe at Lipetsk in Russia. However, the actual build-up of the Luftwaffe began officially with the establishment of the Air Ministry of the Reich (Reichsluftfahrt-ministerium, or RLM) on 5 May 1933. With the introduction of conscription in 1935, the Luftwaffe came out of hiding. The simultaneous announcement of military sovereignty on 16 March 1935 brought together all former civil flying units into the new Luftwaffe.

Among the best known groups was the 'Mitteldeutsche Reklamestaffel' (Central German Display Squadron) which later became the core of Jagdgeschwader (JG) 132. This led to the establishment in April 1934 of the Fighter Training School at Schleissheim near Munich, followed by others at Oldenburg and Werneuchen.

On 14 March 1935 the first fighter group was established as JG 132 at Döberitz with the famous name of 'Richthofen'. Although Junkers and Dornier had already proved the worth of monoplanes in the First World War, the fighter group was equipped initially with biplanes, namely the Arado Ar 65, Ar 85 and Heinkel He 51. New squadrons followed soon after the establishment of JG 132, and made their first public appearance during Hitler's military occupation of the Rhineland. In the Spanish Civil War, which was used as a testing ground for new weapons, the single-engined Messerschmitt Bf 109 and Heinkel He 112 monoplane fighters were tried out in action. At that time further new squadrons were being created regularly.

As a result of forming so many bomber, dive-bomber and heavy fighter squadrons, the fighter force was short of suitable officers. This later proved disastrous in terms of personnel and, because of the limitations of the offensive thinking of the German leadership, in the tactical sense. So, out of some 4,100 front-line aircraft which the Luftwaffe had on charge at the start of the Second World War, only 780 were fighters. Only after the aerial battles over Britain did the lack of superior aircraft with corresponding operational range become clear, if only because they had been almost wiped out by then. The heavy fighter groups equipped with the Messerschmitt Bf 110 were unable to fulfil expectations, and the same applied to the successor models Me 210 and Me 410. All suffered heavy losses as a result of their poor manoeuvrability compared with single-engined aircraft.

The night fighter at first led a precarious existence, since it lacked a suitable operational role. However, with the introduction of the Bf 110 C, the Junkers Ju 88 C, and the Dornier Do 217 J, it could fulfil its role rather better, so long as the Allies did not use their full force.

The first General der Jagdflieger, Adolf Galland, expounded on the theme of fighters and heavy-fighters as follows: 'If the level of fighter production of 1944 had been available in 1940 or even in 1941, the Luftwaffe would never have lost so many men on any front, and the overall course of the war would therefore have taken a decisively different direction.'

With the delivery of the Focke-Wulf Fw 190 A, as well as the equipping of night fighter squadrons with considerably more powerful aircraft such as the Bf 110 G, Ju 88 G or He 219 A, relatively well-developed systems became available to defend against an enemy continuously growing in strength. Meanwhile, the picture had changed.

Allied air superiority had forced the

Luftwaffe into an increasingly defensive role. The appearance of Spitfires and American long-range fighters such as the Thunderbolt and the Mustang (the production of which was totally unaffected by war conditions in Europe) meant that, despite the increasing quality of its aircraft, the Luftwaffe had no chance in the end. This was not changed in the least by either the first rocket and jet aircraft nor the long-nosed Fw 190 D or 'Dora'. Precision bombing of production facilities meant that, despite the immense output of 1944, fighter groups in the West, although by no means lacking in bravery, were no longer able to seize the initiative against the RAF and the USAAF. The devastating air raids on the German fuel industry, as well as attacks on the road network, meant that many units of both and day and night fighters never even reached their squadrons.

The basic error of the German Luftwaffe lay in its unchangingly offensive thinking. New dive-bomber and attack aircraft squadrons were continually being established and presented as the route to victory. The constant attrition as well as increasing Allied superiority, even with little or no fighter support, produced high losses in the crews involved. Well-trained personnel who would have been essential to the fighter force, as the Luftwaffe found itself fully on the defensive, were lost in increasing numbers. Nevertheless, between 1 September 1939 and 8 May 1945, the German fighter squadrons destroyed some 70,000 enemy aircraft. More than 100 Luftwaffe pilots claimed over 100 kills, and indeed Erich Hartmann reached 350. There was however a price to be paid: 14,300 men never returned from their missions.

From the technical point of view, the war had an immense effect on aircraft design. Aerodynamically superior fighters, culminating in the Me 262 with rocket weapons, showed the way to such machines as the American F-86 and the Soviet MiG-15.

M. Griehl and J. Dressel
Mainz/Hochheim, April 1992

Below: The Arado Ar 65E was armed with two MG 17 machine-guns and was intended for training.

The Creation of the German Fighter Force

SINGLE-ENGINED FIGHTERS

Restricted by the economic crisis at the end of the 1920s, the second Four-Year Programme of German aircraft construction between 1929 and 1932 fell well behind its predecessor. In addition to the consideration given to bomber development, four new single-seat fighters were produced up to 1932. These were the Arado Ar 64 and the Heinkel HD 43, followed by the Arado Ar 65 and the Heinkel HD 49.

The two latter types were new designs — the Ar 64 was derived from the Ar SD III, the HD 43 from the HD 38 — but they were still fabric-covered biplanes with tubular steel and wood structures. Their armament was two MG 17 machine-guns. After tests at Lipetsk, they were also equipped with racks for five or six 10kg bombs for attacking infantry. Both aircraft were powered by BMW VI engines. The Ar 65 was an undemanding easy-to-fly machine. Built in large numbers, it was the

Below: The Ar 68E biplane had two MG 17s as its fixed armament.

Left and right: These Jumo 210-powered Ar 65Es were also used mainly as trainers.

cornerstone of the German fighter force after Hitler came to power.

After the success of the Ar 65, the HD 43 was not followed up but developed into the HD 49 with a slender, rounded fuselage in place of the previous box structure. The desired aerodynamic effect was however offset by the poorly refined radiator, open cockpit, fixed undercarriage and unfavour-able junction between fuselage and lower wing. The anticipated increase in perform-ance was not therefore attained on the trial flight of the HD 49 in November 1932. Further development in which the undercarriage and the wing root were modified followed, and the maiden flight of the new version, renumbered Heinkel He 51, took place in the summer of 1933. After construction of the necessary production facilities by Heinkel, many more aircraft were delivered to the Luftwaffe from 1935 onwards, and the Ar 65 was discontinued.

When the Albatros firm went bankrupt, Walter Blume moved to Arado and designed both the single-seat fighters Ar 67 and Ar 68. A new development for the Ar 67 was a layout with the fin and rudder mounted ahead of the tailplane. This feature became a characteristic of all single-engined aircraft from Arado and was an almost totally safe means of getting out of spins, since it prevented the tailplane from blanketing the rudder.

The first Ar 68 was built in the summer of 1933. It was found to be extremely manoeuvrable and to have almost perfect flying qualities. Since the Junkers Jumo 210 engine was not yet available - the first test installations followed in the summer of 1934 in a Junkers W 34 - the Ar 68, like the He 51, was powered by the BMW VI. Although there was virtually no difference in the power available to both aircraft, most fighter units were allocated the Ar 68 in the 1936 equipment programme because of its better performance. This difference showed up in comparative flight trials of the Ar 68 and the He 51 by the famous First World War fighter ace and test pilot Ernst Udet at Brandenburg.

Almost parallel with the requirements for initial training aircraft came the plan for a single-seat trainer for more advanced pilots, which could also serve as a defensive fighter. Development contracts were given to Arado, Focke-Wulf, Heinkel and Henschel.

Arado and Focke-Wulf met the requirements with strut-braced high-wing monoplanes with fabric-covered fuselages. The Arado Ar 76 was convincing because of its precise straight-line flight without the least sign of yawing. The Fw 56 had an unconventional tail layout, with only a rudimentary fin and a very large rudder. Directional stability was therefore somewhat suspect. Heinkel's first proposal for a single-seat trainer was a strut-braced low-wing monoplane designed by Robert Lusser, but this was abandoned in the late summer of 1933 and

in its place Heinkel developed the He 74 biplane, which first flew in 1934. This aircraft however had unsatisfactory flying qualities, in particular a dangerous tendency to pitch down. There were also designs from Henschel, the Hs 121 high-wing monoplane and the Hs 125 low-wing monoplane, but they too were not adopted. This meant that, up to then, the Luftwaffe had accepted no all-metal trainers.

In December 1933 the Technische Amt LC II was given the task of drawing up specifications for a new single-seat interceptor, corresponding to the tactical requirements for the 'Armed Aircraft IV'. The aircraft was to be a low-wing monoplane with retractable undercarriage and of all-metal construction. In February 1934 Arado, Heinkel and Bayerische Flugzeugwerke were given development

Below: Crash of an Ar 68F of JG 134 'Horst Wessel' in 1937.

Left: The Ar 68H, seen here in spring 1937, differed from the Ar 68F in having a BMW 132 Da radial.

Right: Work on the runway of JG 132, with an He 51 A-1 in the foreground.

Left: The prototype Ar 68H (D-ISIX) during a flight at Speyer.

Left: The Heinkel He 51 was, with the Ar 68, the first standard fighter of the Luftwaffe. The first zero-series aircraft carried the registration D-IQEE.

Right: The He 51 B-1s of 3./JG 134 'Horst Wessel' were stationed at Werl near Dortmund in the summer of 1936.

Above: Two He 51 B-1s of I./JG 134 in July 1936.

contracts. Model tests of the Arado Ar 80 followed in July 1934, and of the Heinkel He 112 and Messerschmitt Bf 109 in October of the same year. These early trial dates were met because by the middle of 1933 all three firms presumably had projects for fighters with retractable undercarriage planned and actually waiting for the necessary order to come from the Technisch Amt. Focke-Wulf were asked to tender in September 1934 and came up with a strutbraced high-wing monoplane, the Fw 159, which had little chance against the three other designs.

For the Arado Ar 80 a special method of fuselage construction had been developed with formers and sheet aluminium panels. This structure was basically simple but too heavy and labour-intensive. Further problems arose

with the undercarriage. Expensive time was taken up in various tests, so that by the time the comparative flight trials were made at the beginning of 1936, the undercarriage was fixed but streamlined. This revived the impression that aircraft should be built with fixed undercarriages. During the trials it became apparent that the Ar 80 was easy to fly, but lagged behind in terms of speed because of the fixed undercarriages. It also lost a number of fuselage panels during dives. Arado realized that this design could not compete and therefore abandoned it. However, five test models had been built, one of them a two-seater, and these were later used as test aircraft in various research projects.

Heinkel intended that the wing loading of the He 112 should not exceed 100kg/m² (this

Above right: Formation flight by nine He 51s over the Rhineland, 1936.

figure applied also for the Ar 80, although the Bf 109 had a permissible wing loading of 125 kg/m²) and therefore had to retain a two-spar wing. Heinkel also tried to use the He 70's elliptical wing form on the He 112, which was costly and time consuming to build. The fuselage was of all-metal monocoque construction with frames and stringers. Because the required Jumo 210 engine was not yet available, a Rolls-Royce Kestrel IIS was used to power the prototype. The He 112 V 1 made its maiden flight in September 1935. Flight characteristics and power were tolerable and in December 1935 it was delivered to the test centre at Rechlin.

In February-March 1936 comparative flight trials with the Bf 109 V 2 followed. In these the He 112 showed up badly in terms of power and had to be modified. The resulting He 112 V 7, with modified wings and fuselage, could finally match the Bf 109, but by this time the Bf 109 was already into its B-series, so that the Heinkel design could not catch up. In 1937 a batch of He 112 Bs powered by the Jumo 210 E engine was built and 24 of these aircraft were later delivered to Romania.

The Bf 109 was a low-wing monoplane of sheet metal monocoque construction with flush riveting, an enclosed cockpit and a retractable undercarriage. The locking mounting for the undercarriage support was located forward of the firewall, together with the forward secondary spar and the lower engine support.

The oval-section fuselage had a removable end-piece which acted as a rudder support. The two-part straight wing was of single-spar construction, had a trapezoidal planform and was fitted with automatic slats in the leading edges. All control surfaces were aerodynamically balanced and, including the landing flaps, were fabric-covered. Controls were actuated by push-rods, except for the rudder which was operated by steel cables. The landing gear was hydraulically operated. The self-sealing fuel tank was located under and behind the pilot's seat.

The Bf 109 V 1 made its maiden flight in May 1935 powered by a Rolls-Royce Kestrel engine, and in the autumn was transferred to Rechlin and later to Travemünde, where comparative flight tests were carried out. At Rechlin the Bf 109 V 1 suffered a broken undercarriage as a result of damage to the telescopic leg connections in the fuselage. This problem affected the Bf 109 right through to the end of the war, and led to high losses, especially later with inexperienced pilots. In February 1936 the Bf 109 V 2, which was powered by a Jumo 210 engine, was delivered to Travemünde and made its maiden flight on 21 January 1936. However, it crashed in April and was replaced by the Bf 109 V 3. The comparative flights in the summer proved conclusive for the Bf 109. The test (Versuch = V) models V 4 to V 6 followed, and in October 1936 underwent further testing at Rechlin.

Left: The Ar 76 was developed as a 'home defence fighter'. This photograph shows the Ar 76 V2 (D-IRAS), armed with two MG 17s.

Left: The first prototype of the 'home defence fighter' was the Ar 76a (D-ISEN).

Below: Focke-Wulf developed the Fw 56 as a trainer and escort fighter; about 1,000 of these machines were built.

Right: Most Fw 56s were powered by the Argus As 10C engine.

Right: Only three aircraft of the Fw 56 A-0 series were built.

Some of the next eight test models were powered by the DB 600 engine. At the Dübendorf Air Meeting in Switzerland in 1937, notable successes were scored against French and Czech fighters, which were however of earlier design. The Bf 109 V 13 attempted a record flight with the specially developed DB 601 Re engine and then on 11 November 1937 it reached a top speed of 611km/h.

At the end of 1936 the Bf 109 B-0/B-1 with the Jumo 210 D engine and two MG 17 machine-guns went into production at Regensburg. The Bf 109 B 2 had improved equipment and armament.

With the BF 109 C, the Jumo 210 G-1 engine was introduced. The armament was also modified to include two MG 17s in the fuselage nose and a further two in the wings. Among the equipment for the C-2 model was a test installation of an MG FFM machine-gun in the engine cowling. A few aircraft were built to this design in 1938. The Bf 109 D differed from the C-series mainly in the use of the Jumo 210 D engine. The Swiss Air Force ordered ten aircraft of this series.

Left: A camouflaged Fw 56 at the beginning of 1942.

Left: The high-wing Fw 159 fighter, here seen in its V1 version (D-IUPY), was intended to be fitted throughout with the Jumo 210 B engine.

Right: Close-up of the Fw 159's retractable undercarriage.

Far right: Nose ports for the Fw 159's two MG 17 machine-guns.

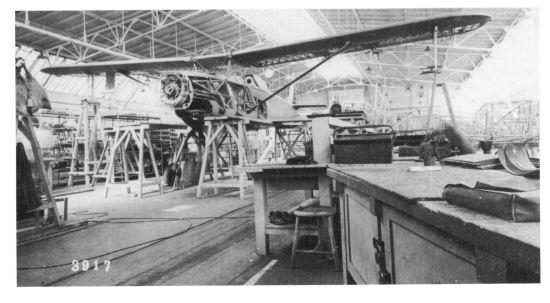

Left: Final assembly of the Fw 159 V2 (D-INGA) at Focke-Wulf's factory in Bremen.

Right: The Fw 159 V4 had a maximum speed of around 385km/h.

Above: In response to the call for Armed Aircraft IV, Arado produced the Ar 80 powered by the Jumo 210 C engine. Shown here is the V2 (D-ILOW).

Right: The Ar 80 V3 (D-IPBN) also flew with a Jumo 210 C engine.

Below: Hans Dieterle (centre) in front of his record-breaking Heinkel He 100 V8 (Works No 1905), powered by a DB 601 ReV engine.

Below right: The He 100 D-1 was powered by a 1,175hp DB 601 Aa.

Left: A typical propaganda shot of an He 100 D-1, armed with an MG FF 20mm cannon and two MG 17 machine guns.

Right: The He 112 V8 (D-IRXO) also had the DB 600 engine, which was built in series from 1934.

Left: Only twelve He 100 D-1s were built. They were shown to a Soviet delegation on 30 October 1939.

Left: The He 112 V7 was powered by a 1,000hp DB 600.

Right: The He 112 V12 (D-IRXS) was powered by a 12-cylinder V-engine, the DB 601, which developed 1,200hp.

Top left: The purchase of the He 112 B-0 was refused by Japan, and the aircraft was therefore offered to Spain in November 1938.

Centre left: The He 112 B-0 was introduced by the Luftwaffe in JG 132 at Fürstenwalde.

Left: The Bf 109 V4 (B-01, Works No 878) was armed with three MG 17s and flew in December 1936 in Spain
.
Top right: The Messerschmitt Bf 109 V3 (Works No 760) was tried out in the Spanish Civil War in 1936.

Right: No fewer than 36 German aircraft took part in the 1937 International Meeting at Dübendorf near Zürich. The picture shows Major Seidemann, Willy Messerschmitt, and Fliegerstabsing (Flight Engineer) Lucht.

Top: This Bf 109 (D-IJHA, Works No 881) was the fourth zero-series aircraft of the B-series. On the right is Dipl. Ing. Franke.

Above: Major Seidemann climbing into the cockpit of his Bf 109 during the Dübendorf meeting, which was held from 27 July to 1 August 1937.

Below: The Bf 109 V13 (D-IPKY) was also introduced at Dübendorf.

Opposite page, top and bottom: Crash landing of a Bf 109 B-0 at Augsburg.

Above: The Bf 109 B-2 was first flown by Jagdgeschwadern JG 131, 132, 234 and 334, and was later used in several training schools.

Above centre: The Bf 109 C-1 was intended to replace the B-2 in service and was powered by a Jumo 210 Ga in-line engine.

Opposite page, top right: The Bf 109 D was first used by I./JG 131 at Jesau. Up to August 1938, about 320 Bf 109s were delivered.

Right: A total of 36 Bf 109 D-1s (coded 6.51 to 6.86) were used in the Spanish Civil War. These aircraft were powered by the Jumo 210 Da engine.

Below: This Bf 109 C-1 trainer was armed with four MG 17s.

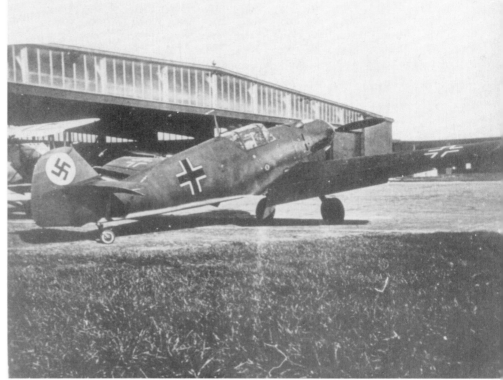

TWIN-ENGINED FIGHTERS

The 'Armed Aircraft IV' of 1934 was planned as a single-engined fighter, from which the Bf 109 emerged, while the 'Armed Aircraft III' was intended to be a twin-engined heavy-fighter (Zerstörer). The Focke-Wulf Fw 187 was planned to be a single-seat twin-engined fighter with two MG 17 machine-guns as armament and a greater range. Kurt Tank developed the Fw 187 without an actual specification from the Air Ministry (RLM). Despite the lack of a general staff requirement, Tank approached the Head of C-Division, General Wolfram von Richthofen, in the winter of 1935 and so convinced him of the merits of this design that he awarded Tank a contract to that specification. In January 1936 the model was produced and in December the Fw 187 V 1 was built. However, the first flight did not take place until April 1937. The Fw 187 V 2 followed in June.

Despite the advances in speed and range, the Air Ministry had no requirement for a twin-engined 'light fighter'. The Fw 187 was therefore equipped with heavier armament and a second crew member as radio-operator/navigator. As a result, the Fw 187 V 3 and V 4 models already in existence were modified to become two-seaters. The next two

Left: A twin-engined heavy-fighter of superior performance was the Focke-Wulf Fw 187 V1 (Works no 949), which was 35km/h faster than the Bf 109.

Right: The cockpit of an Fw 187, which was later armed with two MG FFs and four MG 17s.

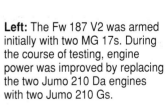

Left: The Fw 187 V2 was armed initially with two MG 17s. During the course of testing, engine power was improved by replacing the two Jumo 210 Da engines with two Jumo 210 Gs.

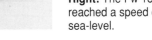

Right: The Fw 187 V1 (D-AANA) reached a speed of 480km/h at sea-level.

test aircraft were also two-seaters. In addition, more powerful DB 600 engines replaced the earlier Jumo 210s in the V 6 model. Evaporative cooling was also tried on this aircraft, but due to the increased weight — from 3,850 to over 5,000kg, because of the need to carry extra water — its range was considerably reduced. In the September 1938 Quarterly Report of LC II there is a description of the Fw 187 as a two-seat fighter with heavier armament and reduced range. In flight tests in early 1939 the Fw 187 V 6 reached the (for the time) amazing speed of 635km/h at sea-level. Despite this performance, the Air Ministry gave the heavy-fighter order to Messerschmitt. Messerschmitt also won the light fighter contest with the Bf 109, although the performance of the Fw 187 was better. Only the shorter fuselage, which did not allow any rear armament, was criticized — a problem, but not an insoluble one. A pre-series of three aircraft (Fw 187 A-01 to 03) was ordered by the Air Ministry and they were tested intensively at Rechlin. In the winter of 1940 the aircraft were loaned to a fighter squadron in Norway, which reported positively. In 1942 the Fw 187 was finally accepted as a night fighter design from Focke-Wulf.

The Messerschmitt Bf 110 did not conform to the requirements of the heavy-fighter programme of 1934 and therefore formed an individual design without

Left: Crash landing of the Fw 187 V1 due to landing gear failure.

Right: Bf 110 B-0 D-AAHI which crashed near Augsburg.

Left: As the standard heavy fighter, the Messerschmitt Bf 110 acted as escort to German mid-range bombers. Seen here is an early Bf 110 B-0 with Jumo 210 Ga engines.

Right: Rear view of a Bf 110 B test prototype for the B-1 (heavy-fighter), B-2 (reconnaissance aircraft) and B-3 (trainer).

competition. Its all-metal cantilever low wing was of similar construction to that of the Bf 109. The forward armament of the third test model was increased to four MG 17s. With its two Jumo 210 engines, the Bf 110 exceeded the speed requirements of 'Armed Aircraft III'. Its ceiling however fell some 2,000 metres short, so more powerful engines were necessary. The DB 600 was not available for the Bf 110 series because of lack of development and production numbers — it was already in mass production for the Heinkel He 111.

Three test models of the Bf 110 were produced and flew in May 1936. In early 1937 construction of the pre-production Bf 110 A-0 with Jumo 210 B engines began. Its armament consisted of four fixed MG 17s in the nose and one manually operated MG 15 for rear defence. This series was later provided with heavier weapons (two MG FF guns in the lower fuselage) and Jumo 210 D engines, to become the Bf 110 B, and was released in the early part of 1938. In addition to the Bf 110 B-0/B-1, there was also the Bf 110 B-3 which was produced in small quantities as a trainer. The B-series was delivered in December 1938. Simultaneously construction began of the C-series with more powerful DB 601 A-1 engines. Immediately after the introduction of the DB 601, production of the Bf 110 in its C/D/E series commenced from the end of 1938. In the summer of 1939 the Jumo-powered Bf 110s began to be delivered to fighter squadrons of the Training and Reserve Groups as trainers.

Left: Bf 110 fuselages under construction at Augsburg.

Left: Test prototype D-AA0V in which the use of 30mm armament was tested.

Single-Engined Fighters

Right: This Bf 109 E formed part of the reserve squadron of JG 26.

Below: Test work on the Fw 190 A-1 at the Marienburg factory.

Messerschmitt Bf 109E

The first two zero-series Bf 109 D aircraft were test beds for the new Bf 109 E series. Flight testing began in the summer of 1938 with the Bf 109 V 14 (D-IRTT) and V 15 (D-IPHR). Both machines were powered by the 1,050hp DB 601 A-1 engine. The V 14 was armed with two MG 17s in the fuselage and two MG FFs in the wing roots, but the V 15 had only the fuselage-mounted armament. At the end of 1938 a zero-series aircraft designated Bf 109 E-0 was produced for further testing. This machine was based largely on the two prototypes, but had two MG 17s in the fuselage and two in the wing roots.

At the beginning of 1939 the first Bf 109 E-1 left the production line of Messerschmitt AG at Regensburg. Only 147 E-series machines were to be built there and the majority of the 1,540 Bf 109s produced in 1939 were assembled under licence at the Gerhard Fieseler Werke at Kassel and the Erla Maschinenfabrik in Leipzig. During production the wing-mounted MG 17 guns were replaced by the heavier MG FF 20mm cannon. In February 1939 the Bf 109 E-1 reached the Luftwaffe's fighter squadrons and was also delivered to Jagdgruppe 88 of the Condor Legion, where it replaced the Bf 109 Bs used in the Spanish Civil War. Forty Bf 109 E-1s were later sent to Spain. The Swiss Air Force purchased 80 Bf 109 Es up to April 1940, but without armament or radio.

The first effect of the opening of hostilities was the realization that the Bf 109's armament and power must be improved. In the early summer of 1939 the Bf 109 V 17 appeared, an aircraft of the E-zero series powered by the DB 601 A engine which had been intended for the Bf 109 E-3, and which could have an MG FF cannon mounted to fire through the spinner. In the autumn of the same year the Bf 109 E-3 replaced the E-1 series. During production, the cockpit canopy was improved and heavier armour for the protection

Below left: A Bf 109 E-1 of the factory defence squadron at Fieseler's Kassel factory, which existed between 16 October 1939 and 7 July 1940. In the cockpit is Anton Riediger.

Right: The early Bf 109 E-1s were gradually transferred to training establishments.

Right: A Bf 109 E-4 of the ErgSt. of JG 26 which was stationed at Rotterdam-Waalhaven.

Below: The Bf 109 E-4 was powered by the DB 601 Aa engine and armed with two MG FF cannon and two MG 17 machine-guns. The aircraft shown here belonged to III./JG 27.

Left: At the beginning of 1940, II./JG 27 flew from Döberitz near Berlin and therefore carried the Berlin Bear as an emblem.

Right: Feldwebel (Sergeant) Richtmann in front of a Bf 109 E of III./JG 27 in the West.

Below: A Bf 109 E-7 of 6./JG 26 in Sicily during the summer of 1941.

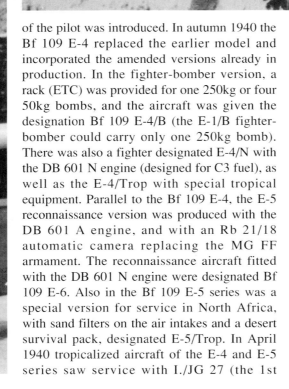

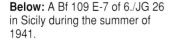

of the pilot was introduced. In autumn 1940 the Bf 109 E-4 replaced the earlier model and incorporated the amended versions already in production. In the fighter-bomber version, a rack (ETC) was provided for one 250kg or four 50kg bombs, and the aircraft was given the designation Bf 109 E-4/B (the E-1/B fighter-bomber could carry only one 250kg bomb). There was also a fighter designated E-4/N with the DB 601 N engine (designed for C3 fuel), as well as the E-4/Trop with special tropical equipment. Parallel to the Bf 109 E-4, the E-5 reconnaissance version was produced with the DB 601 A engine, and with an Rb 21/18 automatic camera replacing the MG FF armament. The reconnaissance aircraft fitted with the DB 601 N engine were designated Bf 109 E-6. Also in the Bf 109 E-5 series was a special version for service in North Africa, with sand filters on the air intakes and a desert survival pack, designated E-5/Trop. In April 1940 tropicalized aircraft of the E-4 and E-5 series saw service with I./JG 27 (the 1st

Gruppe of Jagdgeschwader 27) in North Africa.

A derivative of the E-4/N was the Bf 109 E-7 long-range fighter with a 300-litre drop-tank and DB 601 N engine; it could carry one SC 250 bomb in place of the drop-tank. This too came in a tropicalized version (E-7/Trop), which also saw service with I./JG 27. The E-7/U1 and U2 fighter-bombers had a larger oil cooler and improved engine armour for use as attack aircraft. The E-7/Z version had a GM-1 nitrous oxide injection system for extra power. In the autumn of 1940 came the Bf 109 E-8, a long-range fighter powered by a DB 601 A-1, and the Bf 109 E-9 reconnaissance aircraft with a DB 601 N engine, drop-tank and fuselage-mounted Rb 50/30 automatic camera. In other respects these models conformed to the E-7 series design. A final derivative of the Bf 109 E-3 was the catapult-launched carrier fighter, the Bf 109 T, with the DB 601 N engine which was developed by Fieseler in 1939.

Opposite page, top and bottom: Bf 109 C D-IYMS was used for tests regarding the planned use on the aircraft-carrier *Graf Zeppelin*. The aircraft had an arrester hook and modifications to the undercarriage.

Above: The Bf 109 T-2 was intended to be the production version for carrier operations. It was therefore fitted with a larger wing.

Below: Most of the Bf 109 T-2s built were supplied to 11./JG 11, to I./JG 77 and to the Heligoland fighter squadron.

Messerschmitt Bf 109 F

In January 1941 the Bf 109 F with a DB 601 N engine entered production. Test models for this new series were the Bf 109 V 21 and V 24 (Works Nos 5601 - 5604). The V 21 was powered by a DB 601 A-1 engine and had all the structural improvements already incorporated in the Bf 109 F.

With this series the Bf 109 reached its most advanced aerodynamic form. The new engine cowling provided an almost ideal nose contour, enhanced by a propeller with blades that were both shorter and broader. The wing, with rounded tips and improved flaps, would be maintained in all future versions. The two flaps on the cooler outlet formed part of the landing gear cover. To improve speed even further, the high tail support and the rudder controls were moved inwards, and the tail-wheel was made fully retractable. Fuel capacity was 400 litres, and lubricating oil capacity 36 litres. Armament consisted of two MG 17 in the fuselage plus one MG FF cannon. On strength grounds, wing-root armament was discontinued, but armament could be retrofitted in wing nacelles if necessary.

The Bf 109 F-2 had one MG 151/15 in the engine cowling. When equipped for North African service, these aircraft carried the designation F-2/Trop; the Bf 109 F-2/Z was fitted with the GM-1 nitrous oxide injection system.

The DB 601 E engine became available from the beginning of 1942 and was intended to be used in the F-3 version. This series, however, remained on the drawingboard, and the Bf 109 F-4 was fitted with the DB 601 E-1 intended for its predecessor. The armament was upgraded to MG 151/20 cannon (replacing the 15mm MG 151/15), although the two MG

Below: The first Bf 109 F-1s delivered to JG 26 on the Western Front. The aircraft had an engine-mounted MG FF and two fuselage-mounted MG 17s. The engine was the DB 601 N.

Right: Close-up of the radiator of the Bf 109 F-1.

Right: This Bf 109 F-2 (Works No 9246) was tested with the Rheinmetall Borsag 2 x 4 RZ 65, a 73mm air-to-air missile.

Right: A Bf 109 F-4 of JG 54 in Russia during the winter of 1942.

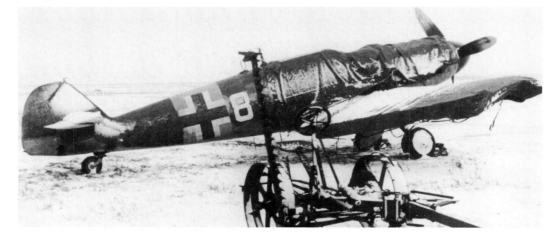

Left: Servicing a Bf 109 F-4 of JG 54 on the Eastern Front. On the underside of the fuselage can be seen the attachment point for a 300-litre drop-tank (Part No R5) or one ETC 250 (Part No R6).

Right: Fitting of an engine-mounted MG 151 which projected into the cockpit of the Bf 109 F.

Left: Close-up of the 1,350hp DB 601 E 12-cylinder V engine, with a clear view of the engine-mounted cannon.

Right: An engine change in the field on the Eastern Front.

17 in the fuselage were retained. The BF 109 F-4/R1 had two nacelle-mounted MG 151/20 cannon in the wings. In the fighter-bomber version the Bf 109 F-4/B carried one 250kg bomb beneath the fuselage. Alternatively, a drop-tank with compressed air equipment could be fitted. For use in North Africa and the Med-iterranean theatre, the F-4/Trop was available. The Bf 109 F-4/Z had GM-1 injection, and aircraft for the Eastern Front had additional cold-starting equipment. The R-4 version (automatic camera) was built for reconnaissance operations. For the fighter-bomber role, the R-6 armament pack for SC 250, and drop-tank or ER 4 bomb-rack (four 50kg bombs) were installed.

The Bf 109 F was manufactured in only a single series of a little over 2,000 (16 per cent of all Bf 109s) before it was replaced by the more powerful and more heavily armed Bf 109 G. In the end, many Bf 109 Fs were used for weapons testing or in further development work on the Bf 109 series.

Messerschmitt Bf 109 G

The wartime requirement for greater power in single-seat fighters, especially after the Battle of Britain, led to the development in the early summer of 1942 of the Bf 109 G with the more powerful DB 605 A engine. With a take-off power of 1,475hp, this engine gave the 'Gustav' a speed of about 650km/h at a height of 6,000 metres. The new airframe featured a stronger undercarriage, a larger oil-tank, the previously available pressurized cockpit, provision for fitting the GM-1 nitrous oxide injection system, rear armour and head protection for the pilot, and roller-bearing-mounted slats. It could also be fitted with a bomb-rack or drop-tank.

As early as the autumn of 1941 a zero-series of several models was tested with the DB 601 E engine. The Bf 109 G-1 was conceived as a single-seat high-altitude fighter with a pressurized cabin. The aircraft went to 11./JG 1, and later a few went to 11./JG 26 as equipment for high-altitude squadrons. At the end of 1942 they first saw action in the Mediterranean.

Series production of the Bf 109 G-2 began in parallel with production of the Bf 109 G-1, and G-2 aircraft were supplied to, among others, Jagdgeschwader JG 2, 3, 5, 27, 52, 53, 54 and 77, as well as 2.(H)/Aufklärungsgruppe 14, NAG 2, and Fernaufklärungsgruppe 122 and 123. Next came the Bf 109 G-3, which was the second of the Bf 109 G series to have a pressurized cockpit. From 1943 this type was used in small numbers by high-altitude

Below: Ground staff at Augsburg. A Bf 109 G-6/R6 with 20mm MG 151/20 cannon under the wings.

Right and below centre: A Bf 109 G-5 of the home defence force with bulges covering the breeches of the engine-mounted MG 131 armament - a characteristic of this model.

Bottom right: Servicing the underwing armament of a Bf 109 G-6/R6 of II./JG 26 in Sicily.

Left and above left: In place of the two MG 151/20s, two MK 108s could be used in underwing gondolas. This photograph shows the prototype for the Bf 109 G-6/U4 series.

Above: A Bf 109 G-6 of JG 53 equipped with a 300-litre drop-tank and two WGr 21 rocket-launchers.

squadrons and by the Ergänzungsjagdgruppe West (Reserve Fighter Group West). From May 1943 fitting of the GM-1 injection system began at Antwerp.

By August 1942 the Bf 109 G-4 was being produced in considerable numbers and this version went into active service in November. The Bf 109 G-5 was the last of the series to be built as high-altitude fighters with pressurized cockpit. With the introduction of the more powerful Bf 109 G-6, the G-5 had only limited application in fighter groups. In February 1943 the Bf 109 G-6 was introduced and from then until the summer of 1944 was produced in large numbers to become a major component of national defence. The first aircraft of this series differed only slightly from the G-4, the two MG 17s mounted above the engine being replaced by MG 131s. It had not been possible to accommodate an ammunition supply within previous engine cowling designs, but from the G-6 typical bulges were incorporated for this purpose on both sides of the forward fuselage.

To improve pilot safety, the aircraft were fitted from 1943 with the so-called 'Galland Armour' with armoured glass, and, somewhat later, with the 'Erla Canopy' (the term

'Galland Canopy' is incorrect). Further modifications consisted of a partial removal of the radio aerial behind the cockpit. In the early months of 1944 an increasing number of Bf 109 G-6s had larger fins with an integrated servo-rudder.

To increase engine power at greater heights, the DB 605 AS was introduced in early 1944; this was a DB 605 A with the more powerful supercharger of the DB 603. As the engine was considerably larger, the cowling of the Bf 109 G/AS was completely modified. At the same time the ammunition supply for the MG 131 was streamlined, and a new propeller was introduced. The first of these more powerful aircraft were introduced at the beginning of 1944 in III./JG 1 and I./JG 5. Part of the older series was re-equipped to AS standard.

The G-8 series was a modification of the Bf 109 G-6 for a close reconnaissance role, and the Bf 109 G-10, which was introduced in the late summer of 1944, represented an adaptation of older aircraft to the realities of air warfare. Using various components the G-type, an approximation to the power spectrum of the Bf 109 K-4 was reached. Since the DB 605 D was not available in sufficient numbers, the DB 605

Left: A small number of Bf 109 G-6s were equipped with the FuG 217 'Neptun' radar as part of the 'Wilde Sau' (Wild Boar) night fighter campaign.

AS had to be used instead. The fuselage consisted of parts of the G-6 or K-4 series, the wing came from the Bf 109 G-2, G-14 and K-4, and the fixed armament from the G-5. The majority of the early G-10s went to Jagdgeschwader 1, 3, 4, 6, 27 and 77. In addition, these types were also found in the three Gruppen of JG 300. After production was stepped up, deliveries were made to II./NJG 11 and I./KG(J) 6. Some aircraft also went to the reconnaissance units NAG 2, 4, 14 and 15.

The Bf 109 G-10 was often used as escort and high cover for Fw 190 combat aircraft, which were increasingly being equipped with 'Panzerblitz' and 'Panzerschreck' anti-tank missiles. From the middle of 1944 some 145 Bf 109 G-2, G-3, G-4 and G-6 aircraft were rebuilt as Bf 109 G-12 two-seat trainers, mainly by Blohm und Voss.

The Bf 109 G-14 was the last model in the G-series. The first aircraft were supplied to JG 4, 76 and 77 in France in June 1944, and later to virtually all Jagdgeschwader. Among others, they were supplied as replacements to Kampfgeschwader (Jagd) I./KG(J) 6, I./KG(J) 27, and II./KG(J) 30, as well as to the first two Gruppe of KG(J) 55. Some of this type also went to NJG 11 and NAG 1, 2, 3, 4 and 14.

Summary of Bf 109 G Variants

Bf 109 G-1 Single-seat fighter with DB 505 A, pressurized cabin, Fug VIIa and Fug 25a

Bf 109 G-1/R1 Bf 109 G-1 without rear armour and bomb-rack

Bf 109 G-1/R2 Reconnaissance aircraft with Rb 50/30, 300-litre drop-tank and GM 1 injection system, without armament

Bf 109 G-1/R3 Fighter with 300 litre drop-tank (production by Erla at Leipzig)

Bf 109 G-1/R6 Fighter with nacelle-mounted armament (two MG 151/20)

Bf 109 G-2 As G-1 but without pressurized cabin and GM 1 system

Bf 109 G-2/R1 Fighter-bomber with 300 litre drop-tank and ETC 500 IXb

Bf 109 G-2/R2 Fighter-bomber with ETC 50 VIIId, no MG 151/20 cannon

Bf 109 G-2/R3 Fighter-bomber with ETC 500 IXb

Bf 109 G-2/R4 Reconnaissance aircraft with GM 1 and automatic camera

Bf 109 G-2/R6 Fighter with nacelle-mounted MG 151/20

Bf 109 G-2/U2 As G-2, but with Me P6 reversible propeller

Bf 109 G-3 As G-1, but with FuG 16Z replacing FuG VIIa

Bf 109 G-4 Reconnaissance aircraft, as G-2 but with FuG 16 replacing FuG VIIa

Bf 109 G-4/R1 ETC 500 IXb for 500kg bomb load

Bf 109 G-4/R2 Rb 50/30, no cannon

Bf 109 G-4/R3 Built-in automatic camera

Bf 109 G-4/R4 Rb 50/30, both MG 17s removed

Right: A Bf 109 G-6 with FuG 217 J-1/J-2 search radar at the Werneuchen Test Establishment.

Bf 109 G-4/R6 MG 151/20 as nacelle armament

Bf 109 G-4/R7 Radio direction finding equipment (prototype only)

Bf 109 G-5 Fighter, as G-3, but with two MG 131s replacing MG 17s

Bf 109 G-5/R1 Fighter-bomber with ETC 500 IXb

Bf 109 G-5/R2 Reconnaissance aircraft with DB 605 A-1 and GM 1   system

Bf 109 G-5/R2/AS Reconnaissance aircraft with DB 605 AS and GM 1 system

Bf 109 G-5/R3 Reconnaissance aircraft with Rb 50/30 (no series production)

Bf 109 G-5/R4 Reconnaissance aircraft with Rb 50/30, no MG 17s in fuselage

Bf 109 G-5/R6 Fighter with nacelle-mounted MG 151/20s

Bf 109 G-5/R7 Fighter with radio direction finding equipment

Bf 109 G-5/U2 High-altitude fighter with DB 605 A1 and GM 1 injection

Bf 109 G-5/U2/AS High-altitude fighter with DB 605 AS and GM 1 injection

Bf 109 G-6 As G-4, but with two MG 131s replacing MG 17s

Bf 109 G-6/R1 Fighter-bomber with ETC 500 IXb

Bf 109 G-6/R2 Fighter-bomber with MW 50 system

Bf 109 G-6/R3 Reconnaissance aircraft with Rb 75/30, 300-litre drop-tank, ETC

Bf 109 G-6/R4 Reconnaissance aircraft with Rb 50/30

Bf 109 G-6/R6 Fighter with MG 151/20 nacelle-mounted armament

Bf 109 G-6/R7 Fighter with radio direction finding equipment

Bf 109 G-6/U2 Retrofit with GM 1 system

Bf 109 G-6/U3 Retrofit with MW 50 system

Bf 109 G-6/U4 MK 108 cannon replacing MG 151/20

Bf 109 G-8 Single-seat close-reconnaissance, as G-6 but with two automatic and one Robot II cameras

Bf 109 G-8/R1 ETC 500 XIb

Bf 109 G-8/R2 Rb 50/30 automatic camera

Bf 109 G-8/R3 Two Rb 32/7x9 automatic cameras

Bf 109 G-8/R5 Two Rb 12.5/7x9 automatic cameras

Bf 109 G-8/R6 MG 151/20 nacelle-mounted armament

Bf 109 G-8/R7 Radio direction finding equipment

Bf 109 G-8/U2 GM 1 system from GM 1 base

Bf 109 G-8/U3 MW 50 system (field conversion)

Bf 109 G-10 As G-2/G-5/G-6/G-14/K-4, FT equipment of G-5

Bf 109 G-10/R1 ETC 500 XIb

Bf 109 G-10/R2 Close reconnaissance aircraft with Rb 50/30 and MW 50

Bf 109 G-10/R3 300-litre drop-tank

Bf 109 G-10/R5 Reconnaissance aircraft with Rb 12.5/7x9

Bf 109 G-10/R6 Fighter with nacelle-mounted armament and MW 50 system
Bf 109 G-10/R7 Missile-launcher (21cm BR)
Bf 109 G-10/U4 Modification with MK 108 cannon, MW 50 system
Bf 109 G-12 Two-seat trainer, DB 605 A1 engine and smaller fuel tank
Bf 109 G-14 Single-seat fighter with DB 605 A (later DB 605 AS) engine
Bf 109 G-14/R1 Fighter-bomber as Bf 109 G-10/R1

Bf 109 G-14/R2 Reconnaissance aircraft as Bf 109 G-10/R2
Bf 109 G-14/R3 Fighter as Bf 109 G-10/R3
Bf 109 G-14/R6 Fighter with MG 151/20 nacelle-mounted armament and MW 50 system
Bf 109 G-14/U4 MK 108 cannon replacing MG 151/20, MW 50 system
Bf 109 G-16 Single-seat fighter with DB 605 L engine

Left: A Bf 109 G-4 was fitted with three additional MG 151/20s for test purposes.

Left: A Bf 109 G-14AS with the so-called 'Erla Canopy', sometimes wrongly called the 'Galland Canopy', and armoured rear protection for the pilot.

Right: Ground staff at the Messerschmitt factory at Regensburg.

Right: Flugkapitän Anton Riediger was with the Bauabnahme Luft (BAL) for the Bf 109 at Messerschmitt in the winter of 1944-45.

Right: A Bf 109 G-10/AS captured by the Allies in Denmark in 1945.

Messerschmitt Bf 109 K

The initial model of the Bf 109 K was produced in the winter of 1943 at the Wiener Neustadt (WNF) factory in Austria. In addition to a more powerful engine, the Bf 109 K was notable for the use of wooden components. Other differences included improved wheel fairings and a higher retractable tail-wheel. In a GL Order of 2 March 1944 it was established that only the K-4 was to be mass-produced. The K-1 to K-3 versions with various armament and engine configurations were cancelled due to lack of capacity.

The Bf 109 K-4 was powered by a DB 605 D engine. By using a variable-pitch propeller with an electro-mechanical automatic control system, which adapted itself to changes in charge-pressure and speed, and an enlarged cooler, Messerschmitt hoped to obtain a speed increase of 20km/h. Armament consisted of two MG 131s in the fuselage and one MK 108 cannon. At the end of October 1944 the first production aircraft were delivered to III./JG 27, followed by IV. Gruppe of the same Geschwader, as well as III./JG 4 and III./JG 77.

By mid-1944 the Bf 109 K-6 with modified armament became available. This consisted of two fuselage-mounted MG 131s, one MK 108 cannon, and two wing-mounted MK 108s. At the beginning of December 1944 a model of this new 'Sturmjäger' (Storm-fighter) was tested at Regensburg. Although, according to a power calculation carried out on 11 December 1944 for the DB 605 ASCM/DCM engine, this series should have had a speed at sea-level of 608km/h, rising to 728km/h at 8,000 metres, it was never produced in quantity. However, during the closing months of the war small numbers of the K-8 reconnaissance version (with an MK 103 in place of the MK 108), the K-10 and the K-12, and the high-altitude fighter Bf 109 K-14 powered by a DB 605 L, were delivered.

MESSERSCHMITT Bf 109 K

Right: The test prototype Bf 109 V31 (Works No 5642, 'SG+EK') which acted as the early test model for the landing gear layout for the Me 209.

Right: side-view of the Me 209 V1 (Works No 1185, D-INJR) which was first flown by Dr. Ing. Wurster on 1 August 1938.

Left: The Bf 109 K-4 (Works No 334175) of JG 51 over East Prussia towards the end of 1944.

Right: The Me 209 V1 was produced in June 1942 and badly damaged in a crash landing on 8 September 1942.

Left: A snowed-up Bf 109 K-4 of Luftflotte Reich during the winter of 1944-45.

Bottom left: Bf 109 K-4 of JG 77.

Below: The Me 309 V1 was finally fitted with improved landing gear.

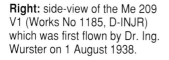

Summary of Bf 109 K-4 sub-variants

R1 ETC 500 IXb or enclosed version 503
R2 Reconnaissance aircraft as Bf 109 K-2/R2 with MW 50 injection system
R3 Enclosed 503 A-1 with 300-litre drop-tank
R4 Wing-nacelle-mounted MG 151/20
R5 Automatic camera Rb 32/7x9 or two Rb 12.5/7x9s
R6 BSK 16 movie camera built into the port wing along with the armament, GM 1 injection system

Focke-Wulf
Fw 190 A

The first drawings of the Fw 190 existed as early as July 1938. They show a noticeably lower cockpit canopy which was later modified. The first flight of the unarmed Fw 190 V 1 was made on 1 June 1939. The second prototype, which retained the Focke-Wulf engine cowling and ducted spinner, flew for the first time on 31 October 1939. The Fw 190 V 3 was never completed but some of its components were used as spares for other test models. The fourth test model was broken up, and the wing of the Fw 190 V 5 was used for static testing. The zero-series began after this version.

The construction of the powerplant installation for the pre-production Fw 190 A-0 was completed by the beginning of 1940, and the series came into production at the end of that year. This aircraft was used exclusively for engine testing and, among others, the BMW 801 C/D, the Jumo 213 (from the end of 1943), and the planned 'unit powerplant' were tested. An ejection seat was tried out in Fw 190 A-0 Works No 0022 in the summer of 1943. The Fw 190 V 7 (A-0) was the test model for the main series Fw 190 A-1. This aircraft was powered by a BMW 801 C-1 engine, which was later used in the production aircraft. The A-1/U2 differed in having the more powerful BMW 801 D-2 radial engine. Four MG 17 and two MG FF were installed as armament in the series aircraft. Production of the A-2 series began in early 1942. From March 1941 the Fw 190 A-0 and A-1 were tested in action by the staff of II./JG 26 at Rechlin. Afterwards, these aircraft went to other groups of JG 26 at Le Bourget. The first air battles between the Fw 190 A-1 and the British Spitfire took place in the summer of 1941 over Dunkirk.

The Fw 190 A-2 was powered initially by the BMW 801 C-1 and later by the D-2 version of this engine. Armament consisted of two MG 17s and two MG 151/20s, plus an ETC 201

bomb-rack. In contrast to the A-1, the windscreen was made of armoured glass and armour plating was added behind the pilot's seat. Production began in August 1941 and ended in the summer of 1942. This version saw service with Jagdgeschwader JG 1, 2, 5, and 26.

Between February and mid-August 1942, the Fw 190 A-3 version was built, with armament as in the A-2 series, although the two MG FFs were mounted in the wings. In the fighter-bomber version, a fuselage-mounted bomb-rack for one 250kg or 500kg bomb, or one 300-litre drop-tank, was available; there was provision for two further 300-litre drop-tanks under the wings. As well as Jagdgeschwader JG 1, 2, 5, and 26, the first

Left: A prototype of the Focke-Wulf Fw 190 with the propeller typical of the early V1 models
.

Above: The Fw 190 V1 (Works No 0001) was later coded 'FO+FY'.

Below: The first Fw 190 was powered by the BMW 139 engine, although this was later replaced by the BMW 801. The aircraft shown here is in final assembly.

Bottom: The Fw 190 V5 (Works No 0015) during flight testing.

two Schlachtgeschwader were also equipped with the A-3.

Aircraft of the Fw 190 A-4 series came off the production line between June 1942 and the beginning of 1943. The most notable difference from the A-2 and A-3 series was a modified rudder with a short radio aerial. The powerplant was the BMW 801 D-2. Depending on equipment, this version could also be used as a fighter-bomber. Most of these aircraft went to Jagdgeschwader JG 1, 2, 5, 11, 26, 51, 54 and 300, as well as — with appropriate modifications — to Schlachtgeschwader SG 1 and Schnell-kampfgeschwader [High-Speed Bomber Group] SKG 10. A modified version of the Fw 190 A-4 was used as a reconnaissance aircraft and supplied to Fernaufklärungsgruppe 123 and Nahaufklärungsgruppe 13.

The Fw 190 A-5 was produced from the end of 1943. In this version, the use of the heavier BMW 801 D-2 engine meant that the centre of gravity was moved forward by some 13.5cm. Armament consisted of two fuselage-mounted MG 17s as well as two MG 151/20 and MG FF cannon in the wings. An ETC 501 bomb-rack could also be mounted under the fuselage. Radio equipment was either the FuG 16 Z or FuG 25.

From June 1943 the Fw 190 A-6 was built in large numbers and differed from the previous models mainly in having an improved wing form with MG 151/20 guns in place of the MG FFs. The fuselage-mounted armament included a further two MG 17s and an MG 151/20 was installed in each wing. During production, as well as during overhauls, a modified undercarriage fairing and FuG 16 ZE

ring aerial were installed. Most of the A-6 series were used in the defence of the Reich. To increase power, GM 1 injection equipment was tested. Some A-6s were converted to night fighters, but their performance was unsatisfactory. For the 'Wilde Sau' (Wild Boar: fighters allowed to range freely and attack bomber formations at will) Divisions, a flare-shield was installed, which made the exhaust less visible. When fitted with ETC 500 and ER4 bomb-racks, the A-6 could also be used as a fighter-bomber.

The Fw 190 A-7 was originally conceived as a high-speed reconnaissance aircraft. However, out of necessity, fighter production had to be increased rapidly, and so from the end of 1943, after the end of A-6 production, series production of the Fw 190 A-8 began. As from January 1944, the Fw 190 A-8 was given additional fuel tanks and FuG 16 ZY radio equipment, all A-8s built before that date being given the designation A-7. The offensive capability of both types was considerably increased by the replacement of the fuselage-mounted MG 17s by two MG 131s. The Fw 190 A-8 became the most important of the Fw 190 series. It differed from the early Fw 190 A-8s (later reclassified A-7s) in having a modified fuselage. The more powerful BMW 801 D radial engine was also installed. Armament consisted of two MG 131s in the fuselage and two MG 151/20s in the wing roots. It was possible to install either GM 1 injection equipment or an additional 115-litre fuel tank in the airframe. Flying weight therefore lay between 4,270 and 4,700kg. Wiring and attachment points for rocket tubes (WGr 21) were already fitted in the production aircraft. From the beginning of 1945 the Fw 190 A-8 had heavier rear armour, a domed canopy and a wooden propeller with broader blades. For fighter-bomber applications an ETC 501 was used. The Fw 190 A-9 was similar to the previous series but could be fitted with a BMW 801 TS/TH engine in place of the BMW 801 D.

In the Fw 190 A-10, a new wing and MK 103 armament were used, but otherwise it was similar to the A-9. Because of the new wing, larger landing wheels could be fitted. Also, in this last variant of the Fw 190 A series, hydraulically operated landing gear and flaps were installed. The A-10 was not a new series but basically a rebuild of earlier versions to a new standard.

Summary of equipment and armament of the Fw 190 A

Fw 190 A-1/U2 Introduction of more powerful BMW 802 D2 radial engine
Fw 190 A-2/U1 Model for course-steering apparatus and turn-and-bank indicator
Fw 190 A-2/U3 Partially armoured close-support aircraft
Fw 190 A-2/U4 close-reconnaissance with Rb 12.5/7x9 and robot camera

Left: Inspection of the Fw 190 V1 at Rechlin (left to right: Lucht, Udet, Franke), Autumn 1939.

Right: Test work on the Fw 190 A-1 at the Marienburg factory.

Left: The Fw 190 V1 was towed back to the factory in March 1940.

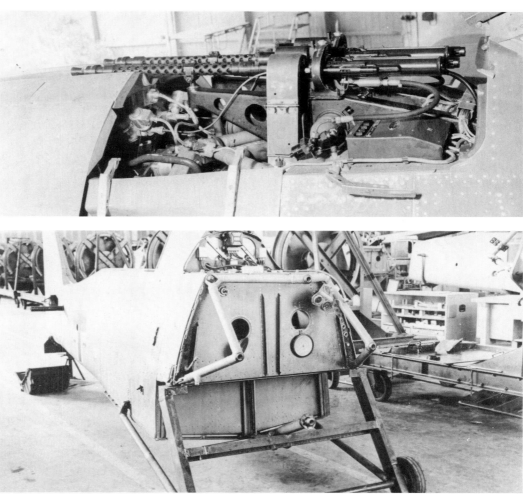

Right: The Fw 190 A-1's armament consisted of two MG 17s mounted above the engine and two further guns in the wing roots. Two 60-round MG FFs could be built into the mid-wing section.

Left: The Fw 190 A-0/U2 (Works No 0010) was initially powered by a BMW 801 C-0 radial engine and later with the C-1 version.

Right: Production of Fw 190 A-1 fuselages at Focke-Wulf's Bremen factory.

Fw 190 A-3/U1 Model for A-5 series
Fw 190 A-3/U2 Test aircraft for introduction of RZ 65
Fw 190 A-3/U3 (a)Model for close-reconnaissane aircraft with fuselage-mounted automatic camera (b)Model for series of six armoured close-support aircraft with fuselage-mounted bomb-rack (c)Sand filter for tropicalized version (1942)
Fw 190 A-3/U4 Reconnaissance aircraft with reduced armament (end 1942)

Fw 190 A-3/U7 High-altitude fighter with two MG 151/20Es in wing roots
Fw 190 A-4/U1 Fighter-bomber with equipment for night operation
Fw 190 A-4/U3 close-support aircraft, later designated F-1
Fw 190 A-4/U8 High-speed fighter-bomber with Junkers ETC
Fw 190 A-4/R1 Equipped with FuG 16 ZE
Fw 190 A-4/R6 Formation destroyer with 21cm rocket tubes

Fw 190 A-5/R1 Equipped with FuG 16 ZE

Fw 190 A-5/R6 Formation destroyer with 21cm rocket tubes

Fw 190 A-5/U1 Nacelle-mounted MK 103s

Fw 190 A-5/U2 Equipped for night operation, formerly A-5/U8

Fw 190 A-5/U7 Wing-mounted MK 103s

Fw 190 A-5/U8 Equipped for night operation, later A5/U2

Fw 190 A-5/U9 Test model for A-7 and A-8 series

Fw 190 A-5/U10 Model for wing-mounting of MG 151/20Es

Fw 190 A-5/U11 Model for MK 108s (Fw 190 A-8/R3)

Fw 190 A-5/U12 Two nacelle-mounted MG 151/20s (Fw 190 A-7/R1 and A-8/R1)

Fw 190 A-5/U13 Fighter-bomber with Messerschmitt ETC (Jabo-Rei)

Fw 190 A-5/U14 Torpedo-carrier

Fw 190 A-5/U15 PKS 11 course-steering and homing equipment; from May 1943 designation for aircraft with MK 103 or MK 108 nacelle-mounted armament

Fw 190 A-5/U16 Replacement of MG 151/20s with MK 108s

Fw 190 A-5/U17 Armoured attack aircraft, forerunner of F-3

Fw 190 S-5 Two-seat version of Fw 190 A-5

Fw 190 A-6/R1 Two nacelle-mounted MG 151/20s

Fw 190 A-6/R2 As A-6/R1 but with two 520-litre fuel tanks in fuselage and one 300-litre drop-tank on ETC 501

Fw 190 A-6/R3 Nacelle-mounted MK 103s

Fw 190 A-6/R6 As A-5/R6, two 21cm WGr 21s replacing external MG 151/20s

Fw 190 A-7/R1 Two nacelle-mounted MG 151/20s

Fw 190 A-7/R2 Fighter with two wing-mounted MK 108s

Fw 190 A-7/R3 One MK 103 in each nacelle

Fw 190 A-7/R6 Two WGr 21 rocket tubes

Fw 190 A-8/R1 Two nacelle-mounted MG 151/20Es

Left: An early Fw 190 A-1 jacked up for undercarriage inspection.

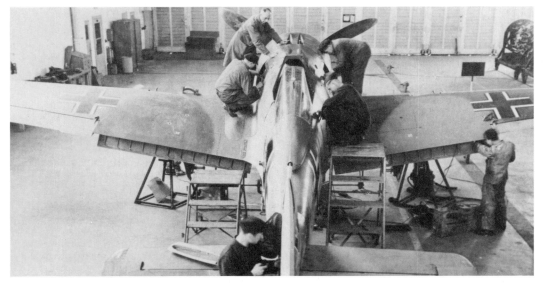

Left: Final checks on an Fw 190 A-1 at Bremen.

Right: Tuning the engine of an Fw 190 A-1.

Right: Ground crew being introduced to an Fw 190 A-1.

Below: With its six fixed guns, the Fw 190 was a formidable fighter.

Fw 190 A-8/R2 Fighter with two wing-mounted MK 108s

Fw 190 A-8/R3 Two nacelle-mounted MK 103s

Fw 190 A-8/R4 Two wing-mounted MG 151/20Es

Fw 190 A-8/R6 Provision for two 21cm rocket tubes

Fw 190 A-8/R7 Fw 190 A-8 with additional armour for Sturmstaffel (ramming attacks)

Fw 190 A-8/R8 Fw 190 A-8/R2 with Sturmstaffel armour (as R7)

Fw 190 A-8/R11 Powered by BMW 801 TU engine, FuG 16 ZE or FuG 125 (all-weather fighter), heated windscreen

Fw 190 A-8/R12 As R2, but with BMW 801 D engine and equipment as R11

Fw 190 A-8/U1 Two-seat trainer without armament

Fw 190 A-9/R2 Two wing-mounted MK 108s

Fw 190 A-9/R8 Attack fighter, earlier designation A-8/R8

Fw 190 A-9/R11 All-weather fighter (corresponding to A-8/R11)

Fw 190 A-9/R12 All-weather fighter (rebuild of A-9/R11)

Top: An Fw 190 A-1 being refuelled at Hannover-Langenhagen.

Above: An Fw 190 A-1 showing the type of cover generally used to protect aircraft against the weather.

Top right: Jacking up an Fw 190 A-1 with hydraulic equipment; this was necessary in order to attach the drop load.

Right: Factory testing by Focke-Wulf at Hannover-Langenhagen in 1942.

Right: An Fw 190 A-1 (Works No 0047) shortly before an engine test.

Above left: Model of a robot camera installed in the wing of an Fw 190 A-2.

Above: An Fw 190 A-2 of 5./JG 26 on the Western Front.

Left: Brand-new Fw 190 fighters ready for delivery to Jagdgeschwader 26.

Left: The Fw 190 A-2 series was instantly recognizable by the cooling gills set behind the BMW 801's cowling.

Right: An Fw 190 A-4 which still has the A-1 series rudder.

Right: Changing the engine of an Fw 190 A-3 of JG 26 on 3 May 1942.

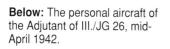

Below: The personal aircraft of the Adjutant of III./JG 26, mid-April 1942.

Below right: Most of the Fw 190 A-series could be fitted with a 300-litre drop-tank without major modification.

Above left: The Fw 190 A-6 could be identified by its four wing-mounted MG 151 cannon.

Left: To reduce the glare from exhausts, Fw 190 night fighters were fitted with flare-shields.

Below: This Fw 190 A-6 with FuG 218 was attached to NJG

Above: Preparing for action with JG 300 in February 1944. The pilot of this Fw 190 A-6 was Oberfeldwebel Löfgen.

Above right: This Fw 190 A-8 was in service with 'Sturmstaffel' 8./JG 300.

Right: Numerous Fw 190 fighters were used as auxiliary fighter-bombers before the Fw 190 G became available.

Below: The Fw 190 A-3/U7 went into production as a high-altitude fighter after only three test aircraft.

Left: The armament of the Fw 190 A-3/U7 (Works Nos 528, 530 and 531) was reduced to only two MG 151/20 cannon on weight grounds.

Right: Front view of the Fw 190 V18 'Höhenjäger II' [High-altitude Fighter II] (Works No 0040, 'CF+OY') which was powered by a DB 603 A-1 in-line engine (Works No 17476) with a GM 1 nitrous-oxide injection system.

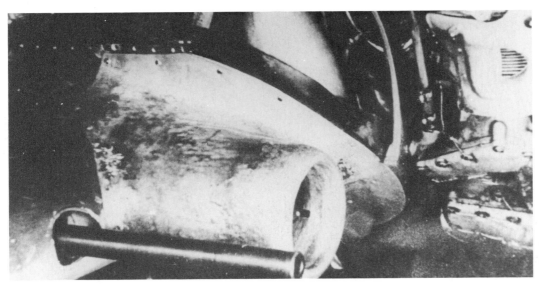

Left: Test installation of a supercharger near the wing root of an Fw 190.

Right: The Fw 190 V18 served as the prototype for the planned C-series. The V18/U1 was equipped with a TK 11 supercharger for extra power.

Left: The Fw 190 V15 (Works No 0037, 'CF+OV') was powered by a DB 603 A-2 engine. The photograph was taken at Hannover-Langenhagen.

Right: This Fw 190 V18, seen in a hangar at Hannover-Langenhagen, was fitted with both FuG 7A and FuG 25A radars.

Focke-Wulf Fw 190 D

Further development of the already successful Fw 190 series began under the designations D-1 and D-2, and these were seen as replacements of all previous designs in the A-series. Production Plan LP 223 of August 1943 specified large-scale product-ion of the D-1 with the Jumo 213 A inline engine at the rate of up to 950 aircraft per month. The first production version with the Jumo 213 A, the Fw 190 D-9, can be regarded, together with the more powerful variants (D-10 to D-15), as the peak of Fw 190 development.

One of the first models of the projected Fw 190 D-9, which had a longer nose and extended rear fuselage, was ordered in October 1942 and from the end of the year was built by Focke-Wulf. Official viewing of the model took place early in July 1943 and the order for full-scale production of a model equipped with a Jumo 213 was given in March 1944.

Prototypes for the development of the D-series were the Fw 190 V 17, V 22 and V 23, as well as the engine test versions V 53 and V 54. In October 1944 the first Fw 190 D-9 series aircraft were equipped with the Jumo 213 A-1, later replaced by a Jumo 213 C-1.

As the Fw 190 D-9 had acceptable operational safety, it became a definite part of the equipment programme. Both the Jumo 213 A-1 and C-1 were available as power units. Armament consisted at first of two MG 131 and two MG 151/20s. Two further MG 151/20s or two MK 108s could be installed in the wings, in which case the two fuselage-mounted MG 131s were removed. An ETC 501 was mounted below the fuselage as a bomb-rack or for carrying one 300-litre drop-tank. Only two examples of the Fw 190 D-10 series, fitted with the Jumo 213 C-1 and one MK 108 cannon, were produced and after tests at

Right: The Fw 190 V53 flew as the prototype for the D-9 series. In the summer of 1944 this aircraft suffered a radiator defect and had to make a forced landing at Langenhagen.

Below right: On 19 September 1944 the V53 was taken from Hannover to Tarnewitz to be tested with an engine-mounted MK 103 cannon.

Below: Prototype of the Fw 190 D with a Jumo 213 in-line engine.

Tarnewitz in the summer of 1944 they became part of the Ta 152 development programme.

The Fw 190 D-11 was the all-weather fighter version of the D-series and differed mainly in the use of the Jumo 213 F-1 engine with supercharger. According to the Factory Summary of 15 October 1944, no series production was planned. At the beginning of 1945 the head of TLR decided to begin production of the Fw 190 D-11 by the spring. The MK 108 and MG 151 armament was to remain. Up to the end of the war there were some seven Fw 190 D-11 models, the Fw 190 V 55 to V 61, of which three aircraft were rebuilt versions of the Fw 190 A-8.

Early in October 1944 the Air Ministry ordered the series production of the Fw 190 D-12 from December with the Jumo 213 E engine and MW 50 fuel injection (later, the Jumo 213 F-1 was installed), and also required the two-stage supercharger to be available, if possible, by November. Armament consisted of one central MK 108 cannon and two MG 151/20 guns in the wing roots. The Fw 190 D-12 could also serve as a torpedo launcher for the D-9 series which was coming to an end. Trials of the D-12 test model (a modified Fw 190 A-8) began in early 1945 with various types of armament. Series production began in May 1945. The Fw 190 D-13 differed from the D-11 and D-12 in having a MG 151/20 cannon in place of the MK 108; the weapons in the wing-roots were retained. Prototypes were designated V 62 and V 71 and were converted Fw 190 A-8s.

Based on the Fw 190 D-9 was the Fw 190 D-14 high-altitude fighter with DB 603 LA engine. This variant was part of the April 1945 Forward Plan. The Fw 190 V-18/U2 and V-21/U1 were used as test aircraft. Both were then used in development of the Ta 152, especially as the series production was by now failing as the DB 605 was already intended for the Ta 152. Much the same may be said for the Fw 190 D-15, a high-altitude fighter based on the D-14, powered by a DB 603 G and armed with two MK 108s and two MG 151/20s.

Armament for Fw 190 D-9

Fighter	Two MG 131s and two MG 151/20s
Fighter	Two MG 131s, two MG 151/20s and 300-litre drop-tank
Fighter-bomber	Two MG 131s, two MG 151/20s and ETC 504
Fighter-bomber	Two Mg 131s, two MG 151/20s, ETC 504 and external 4 Schloss 50 L-2 bomb-rack

Versions of Fw 190 D-9

R 1 'Fw 190 D-9 with special armament' (two 21cm rocket launchers)

R 11 All-weather fighter corresponding to Fw 190 A-8/R11

R 14 Torpedo carrier with unit bomb-rack 504 and Schloss 301 launcher for LT IB aerial torpedo or BT 1000

Versions of Fw 190 D-12

R 1 Fighter with two MG 151/20s and one MK 108

R 5 Fighter as D-12/R1, but with PKS 12

R 11 All-weather fighter, adapted from D-12/R5

R 14 Torpedo carrier with ETZC 504 (Schloss 301), replacement for D-9/R14

R 20 Fighter with heavier armament (MK 103s in wing roots)

R 21 All-weather fighter with MW 50 injection equipment

R 22 All-weather fighter with direction-finding equipment

R 25 Equipped as D-12/R5 but with larger fuel tank

Below: The wooden propeller of the Fw 190 V53 ('DU+JC') had a diameter of 3.5m.

Right: An Fw 190 D-9 was captured by American forces near Frankfurt.

Below right: This Fw 190 D-9 served with II./JG 6 and at the beginning of 1945 was discovered by soldiers of the 69th US Infantry Division at Halle.

Above: One of the few serviceable Fw 190 D-11s available before the end of the war. Armament consisted of one MK 108 cannon and two MG 151/20s in the wing roots

Below: This Fw 190 D-11 (Works No 350158, 'VI+QM') was captured by Allied forces at Bad Wörrishofen at the end of the war.

Twin-Engined Fighters

Right: Formation flying with the heavy-fighter reserve group.

Right: Formation flight over the area between Donau and Lech.

Right: Ground crew servicing the cockpit of an Me 410 of III./ZG 76.

Messerschmitt Bf 110 C

It was not until the end of 1938 that production of the Daimler-Benz DB 601 A engine reached a rate that allowed it to be fitted to all the aircraft types for which it was intended. For this reason the Bf 110 C-0 was powered by the older DB 601 engines. In January 1939 this machine was sent to I./LG 1 for service testing. In the same month production of the Bf 110 C-1 series began. However, the monthly production rate of fifteen remained small, mainly because the 'Stuka Force' was being given priority. By the beginning of the war the Luftwaffe still had only 95 Bf 110 B-1 and C-1 aircraft, of which 82 were in serviceable condition. They were distributed between I./LG 1, I./ZG 1 and I./ZG 76. The remaining Gruppen of Zerstörergeschwader 1, 2, 26, 52 and 76 were supplied with Bf 109 C-1, D-1 and E-3 single-seat fighters. The Bf 110 B-series therefore remained in reserve and was used for training.

Even in the first weeks of the war the Bf 110 squadrons suffered heavy losses, because the heavy fighter was considerably less manoeuvrable than single-seat machines and also lacked rear defensive armament. From then on the Bf 110 was used mainly as a ground-attack aircraft or as a fighter-bomber (Bf 110 C-4/B). Employment of the Bf 110 as an escort fighter, especially in the air battles over Britain, proved disastrous.

At the end of 1941 the C-series was discontinued in favour of the Bf 110 D-2 and D-3 long-range fighter-bomber versions with underwing drop-tanks and fuselage-mounted bomb-racks. The E-series also served as a fighter-bomber and long-range reconnaissance aircraft. With the F-series, the Bf 110 was given heavier armament. The Bf 110 F-4 was used from 1942 as part of the 'Helle Nachtjagd' ('illuminated night fighter': code name for a system combining searchlights and radio-directed fighters) campaign. Produced in parallel with the F-series with DB 601 F-1 engines from mid-1942 was the better armed and more powerful G-series with DB 605 B-1s.

Summary of Bf 110 C

C-0 Zero-series; four MG 17s in nose, two MG FFs under fuselage
C-1 Escort heavy-fighter; series as C-0

Below: Factory test of a Bf 110 F-1 at Augsburg-Haunstetten.

C-2 As C-1
C-3 As C-1, gun turret with MG FF/M
C-4 Armament as C-1; heavier cockpit armour and two ETC 500/IX b; DB 600 A-1 engines
C-4/B As C-4 but with DB 601 Ns; used as dive-bomber (dive angle up to 45deg), Revi C12d sight
C-5 Reconnaissance aircraft with automatic camera; DB 601 A-1s
C-6 Heavy-fighter; armament as C-1 but with one MK 101 in ventral fairing under fuselage; DB 601 A-1s
C-7 Fighter-bomber; similar to C-4/B; DB 601 Ns

Equipment of Bf 110 C

U1 Tow-attachment for glider (C-1)
U3 Heavier armour to rear, below fuselage and around radiator
U4 Heavier armour around engines
U6 Extra armour for coolant equalizing reservoir

Top: During a belly-landing in the early summer of 1940 at Augsburg, this Bf 110 was severely damaged in both engines.

Above: Two Bf 110 Cs of the heavy-fighter reserve group in southern Germany.

Right: Formation flying with the heavy-fighter reserve group. Not all Bf 110s were fully armed.

Right: Series production of fuselages for the Bf 110 D-3.

Messerschmitt Me 210

After the annexation of the Sudetenland (Western area of Czechoslovakia) in the autumn of 1938, the Air Ministry awarded a contract to both Arado and Messerschmitt for a replacement of the Bf 110. The new heavy-fighter was to be faster and to have better armament, especially to the rear. Arado came up with the Ar 240 (limited production only) and Messerschmitt with the Me 210.

The size of the Me 210 differed only slightly from that of the Bf 110, so virtually the only performance gain that could be achieved was range, and this with additional all-up weight because of the greater fuel load. The requirement for improved defensive armament was to be met by the installation of a rotatable MG 131 machine-gun in a barbette on each side of the fuselage. The gunner had a good sideways view through a bulged Plexiglas dome, and the guns were traversed by a servo-mechanism. The crew space was wide with the fuselage nipped in sharply to the rear.

The Air Ministry had already placed its order for the Me 210 series before the maiden flight took place on 2 September 1939. However, this maiden flight showed up the problems of the Me 210. The aircraft proved to have poor longitudinal stability. This was not only disadvantageous for gun- and bomb-aiming, but also dangerous for the aircraft itself. Although this problem became apparent during the first weeks of flight trials, Messerschmitt consistently refused to deal with it by lengthening the fuselage, because this would have involved changing a whole range of components already produced. It would be a further two years before a fuselage extension and a wing rebuild would be made at the order of the Air Ministry. With these modifications, the aircraft showed acceptable flying characteristics and then, after a four-year delay, went into production as the Me 410.

Left: The first prototype Me 210 V1 (D-AABF, Works No 0001), flew for the first time on 25 September 1939, piloted by Dr. Ing. Hermann Wurster.

Lower left: Hold-ups in the development of the Me 210 occurred not only because of technical and staff shortages, but also because of the weather.

Above: Close-up of rudder of Me 210 with Works No 0026.

Above right and right: Nose section of an Me 210 used as a test-bed for the RZ 100 heavy-aircraft armament, which had a calibre of 42cm and a weight of 730kg.

Lower right: The Me 310 originated from an Me 210 A-1 (Works No 0179, 'VN+AQ'), and was flight-tested on 11 September 1943.

Messerschmitt Me 410

The adverse flying characteristics of the multi-purpose Me 210 became apparent during its flight trials. Eventually, two-and-a-half years after the first flight of the Me 210 V 1 (2 September 1939), production was stopped in January 1942. Messerschmitt then provided the Me 210 V 17 with a new rear fuselage. This modified aircraft first flew in March 1942 and showed acceptable flying characteristics. At the end of April, Göring reversed the order to end production, and allowed the Me 210 to be tested as the Me 410 with more powerful DB 603 engines and modified fuselage. In the autumn of 1942, therefore, the Me 410 V 1, a modified Me 210 A, made its first flight.

From this arose the Me 410 A-1 high-speed attack aircraft which entered production at Augsburg in January 1943. The two-seat Me 410 was powered by two DB 603 A-1 engines with provision for the GM 1 nitrous oxide injection system, which gave it a maximum speed of 615km/h. Flying weight was 11,240kg, of which 1,000kg was internal bomb-load.

The Me 410 A-1/U1 reconnaissance version had a camera mounted vertically in the centre of the fuselage. The A-1/U2 heavy-fighter version was equipped with two extra MG 151/20s mounted in the bomb bay using a special WB 151 'weapons container'. From the beginning of 1944, another reconnaissance version, the Me 410 A-3, became available to the long-range reconnaissance squadrons. This

Below: The fixed armament of Me 410 B-2/U2/R5 was four MG 151/20s, which were mounted in the former bomb bay.

was fitted with two Rb 75/30 automatic cameras and MG 17 armament.

By that time the Me 410 A-1 was also being mass-produced by Dornier. In April 1944, production of the Me 410 B-1 was transferred entirely from Messerschmitt to Dornier. This high-speed bomber differed from the A-series in having more powerful DB 603 G engines of 1,900hp each. As with the A-series, there was also a reconnaissance version, the Me 410 B-3. The Me 410 B-2 was a heavy-fighter version. From early 1944, some Me 410 B-6s equipped with FuG 200 search radar were used against naval forces from Lorient in France. In these aircraft both MG 17s were replaced by MG 131s. In addition, they received as standard equipment the WB 103 with two MK 103 cannon. The Me 410 B-5 torpedo-carrying version did not get beyond the flight-testing stage.

In September 1944 production of the Me 410 was stopped because of the need to produce fighters. Even before that the Me 410 was reverting to the heavy-fighter duties rather than the high-speed bomber role it had played hitherto. The reconnaissance version remained in service. In all, some 1,160 Me 410s were produced by Messerschmitt at Regensburg and Augsburg, and by Dornier at Oberpfaffenhofen.

Top: Close-up of the FDSL remote-controlled barbette, fitted with an MG 131. The gunsight is clearly visible through the rear glazed section of the cockpit.

Above: Two Me 410 heavy-fighters of ZG 76 at Königsberg in 1944.

Right: An Me 410 B of III.Gruppe of ZG 76 jacked up on the weapons range.

Right: The remains of a damaged Me 410 B-1 shortly before the end of the war.

Dornier Do 335

The development of the Do 335 arose from the High-Speed Bomber Requirement of 28 September 1942. In mid-January 1943 the Air Ministry awarded Dornier with a contract and on 18 April the official model inspection took place. The twin-engined high-speed bomber first flew on 26 October 1943 at Oberpfaffenhofen with Flugkapitän Hans Dieterle at the controls.

The role of the Do 335 varied frequently during the next few years. In November 1943 the development programme was aimed chiefly at producing a high-speed bomber rather than the heavy fighter, night fighter or reconnaissance versions. In January 1944 this priority was changed. Then the reconnaissance version was given priority over the heavy fighter, followed by the high-speed bomber and night fighter. In this respect, the requirements of the General der Kampfflieger (Bomber Force) were diametrically opposed to those of the General der Jagdflieger (Fighter Force). At the end of March 1944 came the order to hold back the bomber versions and accelerate production of the heavy fighter. Only three months later the Do 335 A-1 and A-2 versions were delivered as bomber aircraft. From the beginning of August 1944, the Do 335 A-6 night fighter was given priority over the Do 335 A-3 reconnaissance aircraft. Again, after only two months up to 26 September 1944, development of the night fighter was postponed and emphasis was once more given to the heavy-fighter version. On 10 October the Luftwaffe leadership changed its opinion yet again and ordered a new series of night

Left: Close-up of the DB 603 A-1 engine fitted to a Dornier Do 335 A-0.

Above: Fitting the rear DB 603 A engine to a Do 335 A-1.

Below: The prototype Do 335 V-13 heavy-fighter ('RP+UA'), produced to the Building Requirement of 31 May 1944, with two additional MK 103s.

fighters. The next month, on 15 November, the prototype for the night fighter version, the Do 335 A-6, became available.

The basic tests of the Do 335 were carried out with two prototypes and two A-0 series aircraft at Rechlin. Up to the end of February 1945 only unsatisfactory results had been achieved: the Do 335 could not reach its design performance at 7,800 metres. The type was equipped with an ejection seat and nose wheel undercarriage. It was produced in fourteen test models and a pre-series of ten Do 335 A-0 aircraft. There then followed a few Do 335 A-1 fighter-bombers, and some more two-seaters

with dual control; the latter had tandem seats for training purposes. Then came a study project for a night fighter. The long-range reconnaissance version Do 335 A-4, planned in the autumn of 1944, was never produced.

At the end of 1945 the Do 335 was discontinued in favour of the Focke-Wulf Ta 152. The explanation was that, up to the beginning of production of the series in May 1944, the Do 335 was considerably more powerful than any enemy aircraft. But only a year later after experience in action it was evident that this superiority had been considerably reduced, especially in the night fighter version. As a day heavy-fighter, the Do 335 had a small speed advantage over the Ta 152, but was no better in terms of range or endurance. Fuel consumption was also too great, and production and repair costs too high.

Left: A two-seat trainer similar to the Do 335 A-10 (Works No 240112) shown here was converted to an auxiliary night fighter.

Left: The Do 335 V-17, a two-seat night fighter, was completed at Mengen/Württ at the beginning of 1947 (!) and flew for the first time on 2 April 1947.

High-Altitude Fighters

Right: The Ta 152 H-0 (Works No 0003) at Langenhagen. With the MW 50 methanol-water injection system the power of the Jumo 213 E-1 engine was boosted to a maximum of 2,050hp.

Below: Model tests of the Me 109 H with extended wings.

Messerschmitt Bf 109 H

In early 1942 Messerschmitt received an order to design a high-altitude fighter in addition to a single-seat fighter for aircraft-carrier service. Because of the heavy workload in the design and production divisions, the construction of two special aircraft was practically impossible, so to hasten development of the proposed carrier version, a Bf 109 G with increased wing area and a stronger undercarriage was selected. At the same time Messerschmitt improved the armament by adding two MG 151s in the wing roots. As an extension to its application, it inevitably became part of the high-altitude fighter project, by exchanging the DB 605 engine for a DB 628 and adding extended wing tips, without a great deal of further development work. With a ceiling of 14,000m, it met the requirement. The aircraft was first given the designation Me 155. Work on this project was carried out in Paris and development took place extremely slowly.

In January 1943 the aircraft-carrier programme was cancelled and with it the application of the Me 155 as a carrier-based aircraft. The high-altitude version based on the Me 155 was passed on to Blohm und Voss for further development and Messerschmitt now turned to the Me 209.

On 23 April 1943 Messerschmitt received an order from the Air Ministry for the 'Me 209 High-Altitude Fighter with DB 628'. The performance of this machine was almost identical with that of the Me 155 high-altitude fighter. However, Messerschmitt received only a verbal order to investigate whether a greater ceiling than 14,000m was feasible. From calculations carried out under this order arose the project P 1091 'Extreme High-Altitude Fighter', with a theoretical ceiling of 17,500m. This was intended to be powered by a DB 603 A with a TK 15 supercharger and a six-bladed airscrew of 4.0m diameter. Armament was to be one MK 108 cannon and two MG 151s or two MK 108s. An initial weight of 6,000kg was envisaged. A second variant was to be powered by a DB 605 A with a 3.4m-diameter airscrew. The airframe was to be that of the Me 109 extended by 2m. The remaining data corresponded to the first P 1091 project.

Since forward planning showed that series production of these machines could not be expected before the end of 1944, it was decided to produce an 'Early-Availability

Left: Model tests of the Me 109 H with extended wings.

Right: Model tests of the Me 109 H with extended wings.

High-Altitude Fighter' by modifying an existing model. This aircraft was expected by the Air Ministry to have a ceiling of between 13,000 and 15,000m, and was designated Bf 109 H. The intention was to build a first batch of 200 aircraft and thereafter reach a production rate of 20 to 30 machines per month. The Bf 109 H was intended primarily as an interceptor for use against enemy high-altitude reconnaissance aircraft; a plan to use it as a high-altitude fighter-bomber was abandoned on static grounds. To save weight, the rear armour was removed, only the armoured windscreen being retained. Fuselage construction was similar to that of the Bf 109 G-6, but with a pressurized cockpit. The mass-produced wing was extended by the addition of a rectangular centre-section and new tips, increasing the wingspan from 9.92m to 13.25m and wing area from 16.05m² to 21,90m². The main landing gear was also modified and, after a few flights, its track widened. The tail-wheel assembly was lengthened by 0.30 m and was non-retractable, and the landing gear fairings were removed.

Below: The high-powered DB 628 engine. This is test model No 19 which was intended for use in the Bf 109 H.

The first aircraft, Bf 109 V 54 (Works No 15708, coded 'PV+JB') flew a mere ten weeks after construction began, on 5 November 1943, at Augsburg with test pilot Fritz Wendel at the controls. Further test flights followed up to 22 January 1944 with test pilots Baur, Schmidt and Lukas. The flying qualities were first described as satisfactory, with straight-line stability; pitch-down or breakout on take-off and landing were reported as very good. The second V-model, the V 55, was used as a power augmentation test-bed, and its airframe also received various aerodynamic improvements. However, this second and last serviceable machine was totally destroyed in an air raid on 25 February 1944. Attempts were then made to bring the first test model up to the standard of the V 55, but this proved impossible due to falling capacity and the commencement of production of the Me 262 jet fighter.

In early 1944 Oberstlt Kneemeyer test-flew the Bf 109 V 54 at Rechlin. He concluded that the flying characteristics of the Bf 109 H in all three axes ranged from satisfactory to particularly bad. This was confirmed by Dipl-Ing Beauvais. Despite the miserable flying characteristics, plans to put the H-series into production were almost complete. Jigs made in Italy were ready by 15 July 1944 and had been delivered to WNF (Wiener-Neustädter Flugzeugwerke GmbH) by November. They were intended for the production of the Bf 109 H-2, H-2/R-2 and H-3 variants.

At the Oberbayerische Forschungsanstalt (Research Establishment) at Oberammergau as late as November 1944, Messerschmitt was planning a third experi-mental aircraft in addition to the Bf 109 H V 54 and V 55. However, the Air Ministry cancelled the Bf 109 H on 18 July 1944 in favour of the Me 262 A-1a/U3 reconnaissance aircraft. The remaining Me 109 V 54 was presumably destroyed in the bombing raid on the Daimler-Benz Stuttgart plant on 14 August 1944.

Focke-Wulf Ta 152 H

The remarkable Allied development of high-altitude bombers with pressurized cockpits caused Germany to develop improved high-altitude fighters. Focke-Wulf received an order similar to that given to Messerschmitt, and Kurt Tank, their famous Chief Designer, produced a design for high-altitude and escort fighters with Jumo 213 in-line engines based on the Fw 190 A. By the beginning of 1942 tests with an Fw 190 were carried out and at the end of September the first Fw 190 with a Jumo 213 A in-line engine flew as the predecessor to the Ta 153 (design with DB-engine). In April 1943 further flight testing took place at the test centre. After correspondence in August 1943, some simplification and alterations were made, and

the type number was changed to Ta 152.

At the beginning of 1944 work started on the first prototype of the Ta 152 H-0 series but was delayed due to staff problems. In March 1944 the factory foundations were laid at Sorau. At the same time an unprotected fuel tank was incorporated in the wing — to increase range, which entailed some redesign of the wing.

The first flight of the Ta 152 H escort version was made on 6 August 1944, but the aircraft was damaged in an emergency landing. Two weeks later the second test aircraft flew, but this crashed on 24 August after engine trouble. At the end of September the third prototype flew, and in the middle of December the first production model — however, not the

Below: The Ta 152 V6 (Works No 110006, 'VH+EY'), a forerunner of the C-0 series, was tested at Langenhagen between December 1944 and January 1945.

Above: Close-up of the Jumo 213 E-1 engine mounted in a Ta 152. At sea-level this engine developed 1,750hp, falling to 1,320hp at 11,000m altitude.

final design (H-0) — arrived at the test establishment. In January 1945 three standard aircraft ('Normaljäger') were ready for flying, although with the DB 603 E engine since the DB 603 L was still not ready for production. At the Sorau factory, 26 further standard aircraft were produced and divided into the various H versions. Aircraft of the H-0 series were powered by Jumo 213 E engines. They had an extended and strengthened fuselage, a pressurized cockpit, an engine-mounted MK 108 30mm cannon, and two MG 151 20mm cannon in the wing roots.

The Ta 152 V 5 and the Fw 190 V18/U 2 were the prototypes for the series of Ta 152 H-1 escort fighters produced by the Focke-Wulf factory at Cottbus from the middle of January 1945, and from March 1945 at the Erla and Gotha factories. Production aircraft had a new wing with six additional tanks, a GM-1 nitrous oxide injection system installed in the fuselage and an MW methanol-water injection system fitted in the wing; each could be used independently at altitude.

Summary of Ta 152 Series

Ta 152 C-1 and **C-3** Standard fighter with one MK 108 cannon and four MG 151/20s, or one

MK 103 and four KG 151/15s; Daimler-Benz DB 603 L engine

Ta 152 B-5 Heavy-fighter with Jumo 213 E engine and three MK 103 cannon

Ta 152 H-1 Escort fighter with one MK 108 cannon and two MG 151/20s, pressurized cockpit, GM-1 injection equipment and Jumo 213 E engine

Ta 152 E Reconnaissance-fighter with armament as in the Ta 152 H-1, photographic equipment as standard in fuselage, derived from standard fighter; Jumo 213 E in-line engine

Ta 152 H-10 Escort reconnaissance aircraft with armament as Ta 152 H-1, photographic equipment as standard in fuselage, derived from escort fighter; Jumo 213 E engine

Ta 152 equipment

R 1 Camera-mount for reconnaissance (installed in E-1 and H-10)

R 11 LGW K23 navigation equipment

R 21 MW 50 high-pressure injection equipment in the wings, PKS 12 and FuG 152

R 31 GM-1 equipment with compressed air and 10.5kg trim weight (H-1)

Focke-Wulf Fw 190 B/C

By the middle of 1942 the Luftwaffe's front-line squadrons had already been supplied with an improved high-altitude aircraft, the Fw 190 A. From the autumn of that year, Focke-Wulf made great efforts to increase the aircraft's ceiling. This began with tests on pressurized cockpits and on the GM 1 nitrous oxide fuel injection system. The next stage was to test an Fw 190 B fitted with a BMW 801 TJ engine with exhaust-gas supercharger, and having a pressurized cockpit and increased wing area. A second series of prototypes intended for the DB 603 engine was designated Fw 190 C. A test series produced with the Jumo 213 in-line engine marked the beginning of the D-series. Work on all three models commenced in early 1943.

For tests on the pressurized cockpit, Focke-Wulf fell back on three Fw 190 A-3/U7 models. The flight tests revealed many problems in sealing the cockpit. From early 1943 the B-0 series began tests at Rechlin. The next two aircraft, a fourth B-0 and a B-1, also had pressurized cockpits and, for the first time, the GM 1 injection system. In April 1944 the Fw 190 B-0 went over to BMW. The B-1 series included the Fw 190 V 45 and V 47 test aircraft with GM 1 injected BMW 801 D engines but without pressurized cockpits.

The first machines of the C-series (V 13, V 15 and V 16) were mainly test aircraft for the high-altitude DB 603 engine, without pressurized cockpits. From the end of 1942 the Fw 190 V 18 became the model for the planned high-altitude fighter series with a TK-11 supercharger and DB 603 engine, although still lacking a pressurized cockpit. The TK 11 was installed under the fuselage. From 10 December 1942 the V 18/U1, designated 'Känguruh' (Kangaroo), went for tests to Daimler-Benz.

From March 1943 Fw 190s V 29 to V 33 with the TK-11 turbocharged DB 603 S engine followed, this time with pressurized cockpits. Some of these aircraft of the C-series were later modified as Ta 152 Hs. Since the BMW 801 TJ and DB 603 engines were not yet in full production, both the Fw 190 D and the Ta 152 versions finally flew with Jumo 213 engines.

Night Fighters

Above: Two Do 215 B-5 night fighters of 5./NJG 5 during a formation flight. The aircraft in the background has an two additional 20mm cannon fitted below the forward fuselage.

Right: A Ju 88 G-1 of NJG 3 which was based at Grove in 1945.

Dornier
Do 17, 215, 217 J/N

The development of the Dornier night fighters proceeded initially in three stages: the Do 17 Z-7 as test prototype; the Do 17 Z-10 as production aircraft; and the Do 215 B-5 with DB 601 in-line engine. The first and, presumably only, Do 17 Z-7 was tested by I./NJG 2, and in fact it was in this aircraft that Oberleutnant Streib shot down an RAF Whitley bomber on 20 July 1940. However, only a small batch of Do 17 Z-10s was built, with nose armament consisting of one MG 151 and four MG 17s. Most went to

I./NJG 2 which had up to seven of these aircraft in service. A Do 17 Z-10 coded 'CD+PV' was used to test the FuG 212 Lichtenstein radar at Werneuchen. With the appearance of improved night fighters however, the Do 17 Z-10 came to the end of its useful life.

The next stage was the development of the Do 215 B from the Do 17 Z, and several of these machines were equipped with the nose armament of the Do 17 Z-10. A successful night attack was carried out by Oberleutnant

Below: This Do 17 Z-10 was used for testing the Spanner night-sight.

Becker in Do 215 B-5 'G9+OM' on the night of 8/9 August 1941 using the new FuG 202 B/C. Some of the Do 215 B-5s flew with II./NJG 1 and 14./NJG 1 in early 1943. Several Do 215 night fighters were equipped with the 'Spanner' night-sight which was built into the windscreen.

In October 1940 some Do 217 E bombers were converted to night fighters and were powered by either the BMW 801 radials or DB 603 in-line engines and were designated Do 217 J and Do 217 N respectively. Production of the J-1 began in March 1941. Peak production levels were reached in May 1942 but production fell off rapidly thereafter, when the Air Ministry chose the Junkers Ju 88 C-6, after which the Do 217 N was first tested in November 1942. The prototypes were the Do 217 N-01 to N-03 ('GG+YA' to 'GG+YC'), which had been equipped with four MG FFs in place of MG 151/20s. The first aircraft without the C-Stand bomb rack was designated Do 217 N-1/U-1. Defensive armament was removed from the N-2 and eventually all unnecessary equipment was deleted.

Following a proposal from Hauptmann Schoenerts, the Do 217 was equipped with upward-firing guns, set at an oblique angle. In July 1942 three Do 217 Js were armed in this way with four MG 151/20s and tests with these

were carried out by 3./NJG 3. The first Do 217 N-2 ('PE+AW') had however already been equipped with improved upward-firing armament, with MG 151/20s, in addition to the standard nose guns. Up to the end of 1943, 157 of these Do 217 night fighters, mainly of J-1 and J-2 types (with Lichtenstein radar) were produced. In early 1943 the Do 217 Ns powered by DB 603 engines were progressively replaced. After about 340 Do 217 night fighters had been built the series was discontinued.

The first Do 217 J-1s, still without radar, entered service as super-heavy night fighters with 4./NJG 1 in 1942. Later, 8./NJG 2, 3./NJG 3, and 6./NJG 4 were equipped with Dornier night fighters. In addition to engine problems, their flying characteristics left something to be desired and the landing gear proved to be source of weakness. However, the Do 217 was more successful as a bomber. Difficulties with the delivery of engines and technical problems with the DB 603 meant that many of the Dornier airframes were useless and had to be scrapped.

In October 1943 many Do 217 night fighters were concentrated in Geschwadern 4, 100 and Schulgeschwader (Training Group) 101, to improve the supply of spare parts. Some of the aircraft were given to Luftwaffe communications squadrons. Other night fighters had their deficient DB 603 engines replaced by the less powerful BMW 801s and were sent to training groups such as Schulgruppe IV./NJG 101 in Hungary. Apart from the units mentioned above, Do 217 J and N aircraft also saw service with Stab IV./NJG 2, with 4. and 5./NJG 3, 11./NJG 4, Stab NJG 100, with 9.,11.,14. and 18./NJG 101, and finally with 18./NJG 200.

Above left: The Do 17 Z-10 was usually armed with one MG FF and four MG 17s. In addition to the Spanner night-sight, it also had a searchlight.

Above: Personnel of II./NJG 2 in front of a Do 215 B-5 in May 1942.

Left: A Do 217 J-1 with FuG 202 radar, the weight of which made the aircraft too slow.

Right: This Do 217 J-1, photographed in 1942 in southern Germany, was attached to a reserve unit.

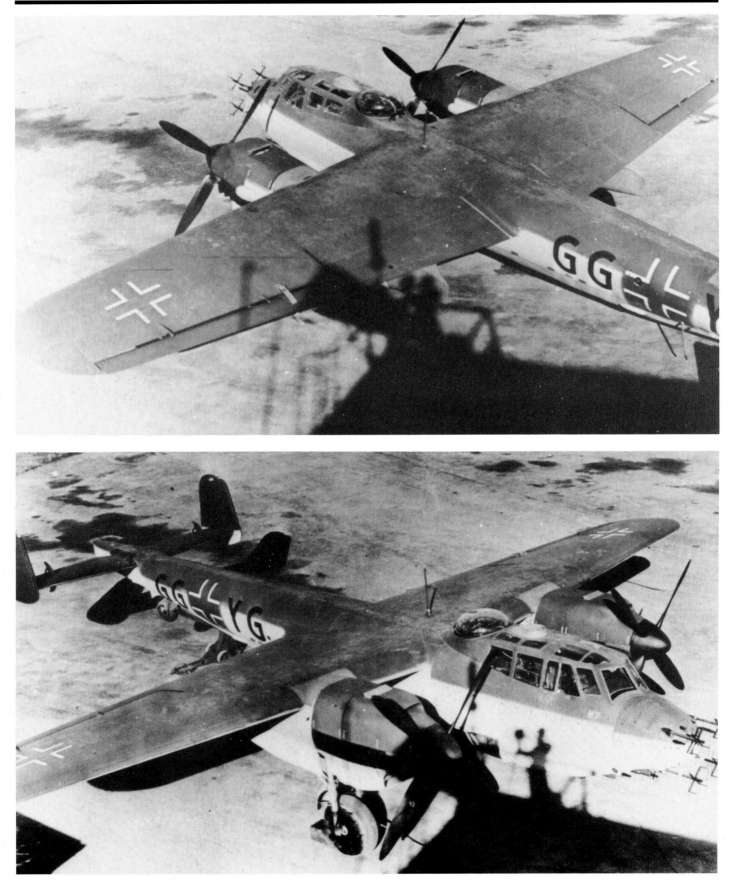

Left: The zero-series aircraft of the Do 217 N-1 was designed as a heavy night fighter. Tests took place at Rechlin up to 1943.

Right: The Do 217 N-04 (Works No 1404, 'GG+YD') had eight nose-mounted guns, plus two MG 131s for defence.

Right: Feldwebel Kustusch's Do 217 N-1 of III./NJG 6 after a forced landing in Hungary.

Left: The seventh zero-series aircraft ('GG+YG') was powered by two DB 603 A-1/A-2 in-line engines and was very heavily armed.

Right: Clearly visible on this crashed Do 217 of NJG 6 is the flare-shield on the side of the DB 603 A-1 engine.

Junkers Ju 88 C/R

Soon after the first studies for the conversion of the Ju 88 A-1 bomber to a heavy-fighter with Jumo 211 B engines, the C-1 to C-5 designs appeared. There was only a single Ju 88 C-1, followed by the C-2 with its five-gun armament. The Ju 88 C-4 corresponded to the C-2 but had two Jumo 211 F engines. The C-5 flew as a heavy fighter with BMW 801 radials. The widely used Ju 88 C-6 was a replacement for the Ju 88 A-5, which had first been planned to have a 'Waffentropfen' bomb rack rather than the C-Stand. The first night fighters had some all-weather capability although they did not all have suitable radar. However, their extensive operational range allowed them to be successful night intruders on long-range operations over Britain and North Africa.

The first prototype of a Ju 88 C with Lichtenstein radar was produced in March 1943 and re-equipped shortly afterwards. At the same time the creation of the Ju 88 C-6 was considered, since the supply of Bf 110 night fighters was not sufficient to meet demand. General Kammhuber regarded the Ju 88 C-6 as obsolete and demanded rapid replacement with

Left: The Junkers Ju 88 V19 (Works No 0373), which was also designated Ju 88 Z19, was tested with additional 20mm armament.

Above: A Ju 88 C-2 of IV./KG 40 at Bordeaux-Mérignac.

Right: The SG 212 aiming apparatus intended for use with the FuG 212 Lichtenstein radar of a Ju 88 C-6.

the Ju 88 G-1. Despite a bottleneck at the BMW engine works lasting for several months, the series was finally fitted with the desired powerplant. From September 1943 Ju 88 C night fighters were equipped with the SN-2 search radar, and the call for more power was finally heard.

In 1942 Generalfeldmarschall Milch had ordered that the Ju 88 C-6 be powered by BMW 801s with GM-1 injection, but this proved impossible because of the inadequate engines. In March 1943 therefore, after several

prototypes, the Ju 88 R-series came into existence. Tests were also carried out on a Ju 88 C-6 with two Jumo 213 engines, which increased speed by 90km/h. However, as this engine was not available in sufficient numbers, it could not be used in service. Similar considerations applied to plans to fit the Ju 88 C-6 with the TK 11 supercharger. These high-altitude fighters remained on the drawing-board.

At the end of 1943 the Ju 88 R-1 and R-2 series entered production. Powered by two

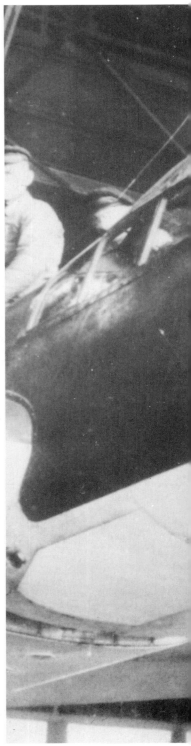

Left: The cramped cockpit of the Ju 88 C heavy-fighter and night fighter can be seen in these two photographs. Note the armament which intruded into the cockpit.

Below: The Ju 88 C-5, a two-seat heavy-fighter with BMW 801 A engines, was only built as a test model.

BMW 801 engines, they also differed slightly in radio equipment and powerplant details. The Ju 88 R-2 series was fitted with SN-2 radar. Some aircraft had upward-firing armament similar to that of the Ju 88 C, consisting of two MG 151/20s. In August 1944 the Ju 88 C-6 and R-2 were still being mass-produced in addition to the Ju 88 G. Night fighters of the C and R series were supplied to virtually all night fighter groups. Both series were finally superseded by the Ju 88 G-1 and G-6. Remaining aircraft were recalled and sent to training squadrons.

Junkers Ju 88 G

As early as February 1942 plans were in existence for the production of 100 Ju 88 G night fighters. In May 1943 the requirement went up to 700 and in 1944 to more than 1800. On 26 October 1943 it became abundantly clear that, just as with the Ju 88 R-2, there would be problems in obtaining engines for the Ju 88 G, in terms of numbers as well as scheduling.

The first G-series aircraft had the nose section of the Ju 88 A-4, the fuselage of the Ju 188 E-1, the wings of the Ju 88 D-1, BMW 801 engines and at first no fewer than six MG 151/20s as fixed armament. Since the nose-mounted cannon tended to damage the radar when they were fired, they were later removed. In one of the first aerial battles between the Ju 88 G-1 and the RAF's Mosquito on 3 December 1943, both friend and foe suffered losses: three Ju 88 Gs and two Mosquitoes went down. The Ju 88 G-1 with the GM-1 injection system was produced in limited numbers as special version R-1.

Its successor, the Ju 88 G-2, included components of the Ju 88 G-1, Ju 188 A-2/G-2 and the Ju 388. Up to the wings and the Jumo 213 engines, the aircraft was identical to the Ju 88 G-1. The Ju 88 G-3 provided an interim solution before the availability of the Jumo 213 E. This night fighter had the Ju 88 A-4 wing and was powered by two DB 603 E engines. Only one prototype, the Ju 88 V 105 (Works No 710523) was built. The Ju 88 G-4 was a heavy fighter with Jumo 213 A engines but did not go into production. The Ju 88 G-5 was cancelled on 2 March 1944 since production of the Ju 88 G-2 was expected in the near future.

Apart from the Ju 88 G-1, the G-6 series was the only one to go into large-scale production. The mass-produced aircraft had four forward-firing MG 151s and two 'Schräge Musik' mountings ('slanting or Jazz music': code-name for dorsally mounted guns intended to fire upwards into bomber formations). Apart from the powerplant it was virtually identical to the Ju 88 G-1. Most of the series were fitted with FuG 220 radar. At the end of 1944 several Ju 88 G-6 prototypes were tried out with the Morgenstern aerial array and 'Berlin Gerät'.

The G-7 was an extension of the G-6 series and had Ju 188 wings and Jumo 213 E engines with extra injection (MW 50) and four-bladed propellers.

In addition to the Ju 88 G-7 high-performance night fighter, a special 'Mosquito-destroyer' was produced in limited numbers. The first two prototypes were delivered on 6 November 1944 but before they could fly they were destroyed in a night bombing raid on Dessau on 7/8 March 1945. Two further examples were still being worked on in April 1945. The last of the Ju 88 G series was assembled at Merseburg in early 1945 and designated Ju 88 G-10. Intended as long-range night fighters, these aircraft were used mainly in connection with the 'Mistel' composite aircraft programme at the end of the war.

Above: Only the first few aircraft of the Ju 88 G-1 series were fitted with six MG 151/20s as fixed armament. Four guns were more usual in later models.

Right: This Ju 88 G-6, attached to 7./NJG 100, had only one MG 151/20 as fixed armament. The MG 131 fitted in the dorsal position was equipped with a flare-shield.

Left: A Ju 88 G-1 of NJG 3 equipped with FuG 220 radar.

Right: A Ju 88 G-1 (Works No 713521) at the end of the war.

Messerschmitt Bf 110 C/F/G

At the beginning of the war the heavy fighter (Zerstörer) was a completely new concept in armed aircraft, with major roles as escort for bombers and support for ground troops. However, due to its tactical inferiority to single-engined enemy fighters, as the war progressed the Bf 110 was used increasingly as a night fighter. Deliveries of the Bf 110 C-1 with DB 601 A-1 engines began in 1940. The C-2 series had MG FF cannon replacing the two nose-mounted MG 151/20 guns. The first victories over enemy four-engined bombers took place on the night of 10 April 1941 (Short Stirling) and 24 June of the same year (Handley Page Halifax). Their power advantage over their opponents was in fact very small. In February 1941, Bf 110 production reached its peak but from January 1942 fell to zero, since by then the night fighter version of the Me 210 was coming on line. In the summer of 1942 losses were still barely

being replaced. Improved types such as the Bf 110 F-2/F-3 with DB 601 F engines and three-man crews, with upward-firing weapons and enlarged rudders, finally reached the Geschwadern.

From 1943 the Bf 110 was seen as only a temporary solution, while waiting for the more powerful Heinkel He 219. Meanwhile, new Bf 110 night fighters had reached the production stage, such as the G-2 equipped with two MG 151s and four nose-mounted MG 17s. As additional armament either two MG 151s or BK 3.7 37mm cannon could be fitted beneath the fuselage. Deliveries of the considerably improved Bf 110 G with DB 605 B-1 engines began in 1942. Parallel to this came the F-series not much more than a year later. The Bf 110 G-1 was produced in only small numbers and was followed by the G-2 series as a heavy fighter and tank destroyer. Fixed armament consisted of four MG 17s and two MG

Right: The Bf 110 V4 of 14./NJG 5 was, up to April 1944, equipped with FuG 212 radar.

Below: These Bf 110 G-4/R1s (coded 'D5+LT') fitted with Lichtenstein BC airborne radar flew with NJG 3.

151/20s, with additional armament type M 1 with two MG 151/20s in fuselage turrets, or type M 2 with WGr 21 rocket-launchers under the wings. This version could be used as a fighter-bomber.

At the same time came the gradual replacement of the inadequate MG 17s by heavier MK 108 cannon. A model with the new armament configuration was produced by the Gothaer Waggonfabrik. The first prototypes were credited with 32 victories while serving with IV./Nachtjagdgeschwader 1 between 2 April and 27 May 1944. Within the Bf 110 G-3 series there was also a reconnaissance aircraft and fighter-bomber with photographic equipment and provision for a bomb rack.

The Bf 110 G-4 night fighter was powered by two DB 603 engines. For navigation it was equipped with the FuG 16 ZE with APZA-6 direction finder, and as recognition radar the FuG 25 A and the FuG 220 Lichtenstein equipment. An increase in rudder size was necessary to compensate for the Lichtenstein's aerial array. Armament and fuel system were largely similar to those of the G-2 series, with the MG 151/20s often favoured as the upward-firing armament. No suitable place could then be found for the MG 81 Z rear defence machine-guns.

The limits of performance were reached with the Bf 110 G-4/U7 night fighter, which had SN 2 radar, a GM 1 nitrous oxide injection system and its fuselage extended by 0.6m. Test

Right: Feldwebel Kustusch of 6./NJG 2 in front of his 'R4+BP'.

flights were made by NJG 1. In many cases the upward-firing MG 151s were replaced by MG FF cannon, as these were readily available. In 1943 practical tests took place with several 30mm weapons, the MK 101 and nose armament consisting of two MK 108s and one MK 103. One prototype flew between August and December 1943.

Most Bf 110 C aircraft served with NJG 1 and 3, with F and G models going to NJG 2, 3, 5 and 6. The Bf 110 G also served with Air Observation Squadrons 1 to 7 as well as night fighter squadrons in Norway and Finland.

Left: The Bf 110 G-4/R4 had four nose-mounted MG 151/20 cannon in place of two MK 108s. This aircraft, seen in the summer of 1944, was attached to 5./NJG 5.

Right: A Bf 110 G-4 attached to IV./NJG

Right: Several Bf 110 G-4s of NJG 2 were given an additional armoured windscreen to provide more protection for the pilot.

Right: Two Bf 110 G-4/R3s of 7./NJG 3, equipped with FuG 220 radar.

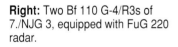

Left: Cockpit interior of a Bf 110 G-4 with a magazine (MG FF) for the upward-firing cannon.

Right: This Bf 110 G-4 ('B4+KA') was attached to a night fighter squadron in Norway.

Left: Night fighter of IV./NJG 2 with clearly visible flare-shields on the sides of the engines.

Right: Service aircraft of II./ZG 1 (later III./ZG 76) jacked up for gun tests at the butts.

Left: Well camouflaged aircraft parks became a necessity during the Allied air attacks from 1944. The aircraft in this case is a Bf 110 G-4 of NJG 1.

Right: A Bf 110 F-2 of ZG 26 with an MG 81Z machine-gun for rear defence.

Above left: Training flight over southern Germany in summer 1942.

Left: Service aircraft of ZG 1 ('2J+AR') for use as a fighter-bomber with fuselage-mounted ETC.

Above: The aircraft park of Zerstörergeschwader ZG 1.

Above right: Servicing the nose armament which consisted of two MG FFs and four MG 17s, at Augsburg.

Right: A jacked-up Bf 110 C-3 of ZG 26.

Below right: Aircrew of ZG 26.

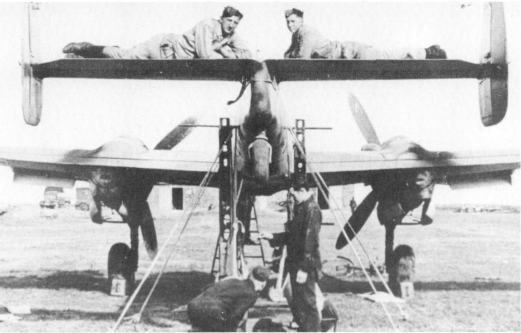

Above: A Bf 110 G-2/R2 of I./ZG 76 armed with WGr 21 rocket-launchers during the defence of the Reich, in which the squadron incurred heavy losses.

Left: This Bf 110 G-2 of 7./ZG 26 is also equipped with a WGr 21 rocket-launcher, in this case with only two tubes.

Left: Factory testing of the Bf 110's ZFR 3 sight.

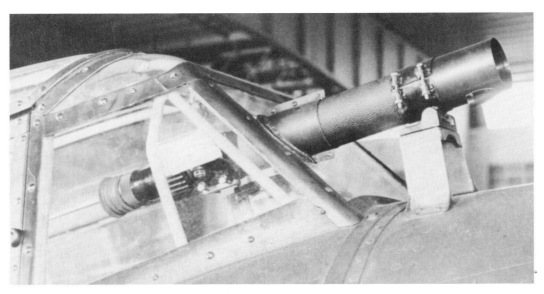

Right: Test installation of an MG 131 for rear defence.

Right: A Bf 110 G-2/R4 with two MG 151/20s in place of the previous nose armament, as well as a 37mm cannon mounted beneath the fuselage, seen at Munich-Riem in June 1944).

Below: A Bf 110 G-2 of the heavy-fighter reserve group.

Heinkel He 219

As early as August 1940 the Heinkel design office was planning several versions of a new twin-engined aircraft including a high-speed bomber (Project P 1056) and a reconnaissance aircraft (P 1055), to which was soon added, on the order of the Air Ministry, a multi-seat high-altitude reconnaissance aircraft. Later the project was continued as 'Reconnaissance Plane' and 'Day Bomber'. In November 1940 a heavy-fighter variant was introduced. This aircraft was intended to have a defensive armament consisting of up to eight movable and two fixed guns. By the beginning of 1941 there was also a heavily armed escort fighter version, and in the summer of 1941 a night fighter version was developed.

In August 1941 the design was given the designation He 219. A few months later, in November, the Chancellor himself was able to inspect the first model via the Air Ministry. On 7 April 1942 the final model inspection took place. The components were produced up to September and final assembly of the first prototype began. Before this, the decision had already been taken to concentrate the whole of

Below: The He 219 A-053 was similarly equipped to the A-5/R1, with the addition of FuG 212 and FuG 220 radar.

the He 219 development programme at Vienna-Schwechat.

After initial taxiing trials, test pilot Peter took the He 219 V 1 model ('VG+LW') on its first flight on 6 November 1942, and on 10 January 1943 the V 2 ('GG+WG') flew. Service units began to receive the He 219 in March 1943, but the intended remote-controlled defensive armament was removed and the airframe extended. Because of the increased length and the enlarged twin rudders, stability about the main axis was poor, there was vibration in both fuselage and rudder, and

severe changes in trim occurred when the landing flaps were extended. Prototypes V 7 to V 9 went for service testing to Venlo in Holland and the zero-series aircraft began to appear from July 1943. The He 219 V 9 began to see tough service from June 1943.

However, a fully equipped He 219 Gruppe remained an illusion at first, as did the 2,000 He 219s which had been ordered, or the rapid transfer from the zero-series to the He 219 A-2. Even Professor Heinkel's vehement demands for more qualified workers for the series production were not enough; in August 1943

Right: Final assembly of an He 219 A-0.

monthly output was still only ten night fighters.

Meanwhile, however, the first He 219 A-5 became available and its armament and performance were convincing. At NJG 1 in Venlo (Commander Hauptmann Meurer) the He 219 was given an extremely good report. Because of cutbacks, the aircraft could not be armed with the intended MK 103 and MK 108, so the readily available MG 151 was used instead. In July 1944 the first He 219 A-7 was given service trials. The B and C series remained on the drawing-board except for test aircraft. The He 219 D and E did not reach the project stage.

Versions worth mentioning include the He 219 V 18 with four-bladed propellers and Jumo 222 A/B engines, and the He 219 V 28 ('VO+BC') and V 31 ('DV+DB') with braking parachute for landing. An ejection seat was tested in He 219 V 6, which was later given Works No 190113 ('DV+DI'). On 19 November 1942 General Kammhuber allowed himself to be shot to a height of 4m at 6g acceleration on a ground rig in order to gain an impression of the Heinkel ejection seat.

The trial objectives of test aircraft were often changed. So, for example, an A-0/R-6 was first used as the test model designated He 219 V 16, followed by an A-5 which had an SN-2 radar system. Eventually these aircraft and the V 19 were fitted with upward-firing weapons and given to NJG 1. The V 28 ('RL+AH') was the forerunner of the He 219 A-5/R-3, and the aircraft arrived at Venlo in June 1944. For the prototype trials it was fitted with DB 603 G engines, and in July 1944 the V 25 flew as a three-seat A-5/R-4.

During the same month Director Francke gave the following results of power trials: maximum speed of the He 219 with DB 603 A engines, SN-2 aerial and flare-suppression equipment (Fla-V-Anlage), was around 585km/h. Heinkel hoped for a further improvement in performance with the installation of more powerful engines. However, the Jumo 222 was not available in series production, and there were numerous problems with both the DB 603 L and the Jumo 213 with MW 50 injection.

A maximum speed of 620km/h at 7,500m had been attained using Jumo 222 A/B engines. With Jumo 222 E/Fs and improved Lichtenstein aerials, maximum speed was to be increased by 46km/h at 11,500m fully pressurized altitude. It was also hoped to obtain an additional 5 per cent power increase by the use of methanol-water injection, although only at greater altitudes. In the event, the A-2 with Jumo 213 Es derived from the standard engine achieved only 635km/h, and as little as 605km/h without methanol injection. The use of this engine also involved considerable structural alterations to the mountings, cowling, exhaust and lubrication system, as well as to the fuel tank connections. Finally, six machines were equipped with Jumo 213 Es with methanol injection by the end of 1944, although the Junkers engine factory was having problems with the supercharger. Because of overloading of the supercharger drive gear, supply to service units was a long way off even at the beginning of 1945. Without methanol injection the power was not significantly higher than with DB 603 engines, so it was never possible for the He 219 to reach performance levels comparable with those of the Mosquito.

During the period 1943 to March 1945, Heinkel produced 268 aircraft of the He 219 series as so-called 'newbuildings'. A further six machines were assembled from surplus parts. Some 27 night fighters which had suffered considerable damage were refitted and returned to active service. The Luftwaffe received only 195 He 219s, most of which went to NJG 1; the remaining machines were used mainly for test purposes or were lost in enemy air attacks. In combat, 46 He 219s were destroyed and a further seventeen were badly damaged.

The A-0 version, with over 100 aircraft, was the most numerous of the He 219 series. As a night fighter with greater range, the He 219 A-2 came into use in quite large numbers. Further, according to a plan of 22 December 1944, 210 of the A-7 series were to be built between December 1944 and July 1945. The first five of these aircraft were to have DB 603 Aa engines and the rest the more powerful DB 603 E. In fact, only a few He 219 A-7s were ever produced.

Despite the relatively small numbers available, the He 219 night fighter was remarkably effective. Altogether 111 enemy aircraft were shot down by He 219s between 12 June 1943 and 25 June 1944. The first major use of the He 219 was by NJG 1 at Venlo, which had already tested the V 7 and V 9 models in May 1943 (by XII. Fliegerkorps). Up to 6 November 1944, I./NJG 1 itself claimed more than 130 kills, of which however only eleven were Mosquitoes.

Above: An He 219 ready for delivery from the Heinkel factory at Oranienburg.

Summary of the He 219

Model	Equipment	Engines	Armament	Radar
A-0/R1	Fuselage extension for V model, normal wing, two-man cockpit	DB603A	2 MK 108s in ventral tray, 2 MG 151s in wing roots, conversion packs M1-M3	FuG 212 C1
A-0/R2	As A-0/R1, stronger undercarriage	DB603A	4 MK 103s in ventral tray	Fug 212 C1
A-0/R3	Model for A-2 series, improved A-0	DB603A	4 MK 103s in ventral tray, 2 MG 151s in wing roots	FuG 212 C2
A-0/R6	Model for A-5 series	DB 603A	4 MK 108s in ventral tray, 2 MG 151s in wing roots, 2 upward-firing MK 108s, Conversion packs M1-M3	FuG 212 and FuG 220
A-1	Planned main series for A-0, recessed two-man cockpit	DB 603A/B		

Model	Equipment	Engines	Armament	Radar
A-2/R1	Improved A-0, single-core wiring, two-man cockpit, extra range	DB 603A/B	2 MK 103s in ventral tray, 2 MG 151s in wing roots, 2 Upward-firing MK 108s	FuG 220
A-2/R2	As A-2/R1, test on flare-suppressor	DB 603A/B	As A-2/R1	FuG 220
A-3	Further development of A-2 with 900-litre drop-tank, minimum standard equipment, two-man cockpit, planned bomber	DB 603E/F DB 603 G	2 MK 108s in wing roots. Planned for upward-firing armament	
A-4	Further development of A-2 as Mosquito-killer and reconnaissance aircraft less armour and armament, GM-1 + turbocharger, two-man cockpit	DB 603A/B Jumo 222	2 MK 108s in wing roots, 2 MK 103s in ventral tray	
A-5/R1	Further development of A-3, earlier designation A-0/R6	DB 603A	2 MG 151s in wing roots, 2 MK 108s in ventral tray, 2 upward-firing Mk 108s	FuG 212 and FuG 220
A-5/R2	Prototype for A-7/R4	DB 603A	2 MG 151s in wing roots, 2 MG 151s in ventral tray 2 upward-firing MK 108s	FuG 220

Left: The first Heinkel He 219 (Works No 219001, 'VG+LW') was used mainly for flight testing.

Model	Equipment	Engines	Armament	Radar
A-5/R3	Series design based on He 219 V 28	DB 603E	2 MG 151s in wing roots, 2 MG 103s in ventral tray, 2 upward-firing MK 108s	FuG 220
A-5/R4	Development of A-3 with three-man cockpit, extra range, defensive armament based on He 219 V 34	DB 603E	2 MG 151s in wing roots, 2 MG 151s in ventral tray, 2 upward-firing MK 108s, Defensive armament in turret possible	FuG 220
A-6	Unarmoured version of He 219 A-2	DB 603E	2 MG 151s in wing roots, 2 MG 151s in ventral tray	FuG 220
A-7/R1	Improved series design based on He 219 V 25	DB 603G	2 MK 108s in wing roots, 2 MG 151s and 2 MK 103s in ventral tray	FuG 220
A-7/R2	Series version with upward-firing armament; proto-type: He 219 V 26	DB 603G	Armament as A-7/R1 with 2 upward-firing MK 108s	FuG 220
A-7/R3	Pre-series for planned B-1 series; prototype: He 219 V 27	DB 603G	2 MG 151s in wing roots, 2 MG 151s in ventral tray, 2 MK 108s as upward-firing armament in fuselage	FuG 220
A-7/R4	Design with reduced armament	DB 603G	2 MG 151s in wing roots, 2 MG 151s in ventral tray	FuG 220
A-7/R5	Mosquito-destroyer with methanol injection system	Jumo 213E	2 MG 151s in wing roots, 2 MG 151s in ventral tray	
A-7/R6	Test-bed for Jumo 222A; prototype: He 219 V 18	Jumo 222A	2 MG 151s in wing roots, 4 MK 108s in ventral tray	

Left: Close-up of the nose-wheel of an He 219 A-0.

Above: Crash of the He 219 V2 ('GG+WG'), which flew for the first time on 10 January 1943.

Below: Two MG 151/20 cannon in the wing roots of an He 219 A-0.

Focke-Wulf Ta 154

After the heavy nightly air raids by the RAF in the early summer of 1942, the German Air Ministry ordered the building of a more powerful night fighter. Heinkel, Focke-Wulf and Junkers were asked to produce a design for a two-seat all-weather night fighter with an endurance of two to three hours and armament consisting of four forward-firing cannon. The aircraft was to be built as a small series with the simplest possible construction, and was to use minimal amounts of steel and aluminium. By using existing mass-produced engines, the first flight was required to be made within twelve months.

In September 1942 Kurt Tank, Chief Designer of Focke-Wulf, produced a design for a two-seat night fighter made entirely from wood and with a nose wheel undercarriage. Two months later he received an order 'With Maximum Urgency' from the Technical Division. Direct competitors to the Ta 154 were the He 219 and Ju 388 J. On 1 July 1943 the Ta 154 V 1 made its first flight at Hannover-Langenhagen with Hans Sander as test pilot. Without equipment or armament the aircraft reached a speed of 635km/h at an altitude of 6,000m using Jumo 211 engines - the Jumo 213 was still not available. Later the machine was armed first with two MG 151/20s and two MK 108s. To obtain reliable values for the stiffness of the forward fuselage and cockpit area, 'barge tests' (underwater drag-testing) were carried out in Lake Alatsee near Füssen by the Luftfahrt-Forschungsanstalt Graf

Right: Wind-tunnel model of the Focke-Wulf Ta 154 heavy fighter/night fighter.

Below: Side-view of the Ta 154 V-1. Only twelve prototypes of the Ta 154, together with a few series aircraft and five spare airframes, were produced.

Zeppelin (FGZ) Research Establishment.

The second prototype was fitted with FuG 212 'Lichtenstein C-1' radar, and was also used for flight testing to obtain additional static vibration data. The first pre-production aircraft, the Ta 154 V 3 (Ta 154 A-03/U1), was powered by Jumo 213 A engines. Because of the weight of armament and equipment, and the full radar installation with four nose-mounted aerials, the top speed dropped by 75km/h despite the higher engine power. Nevertheless, an order was placed for over 250 Ta 154 A-1 aircraft.

Towards the end of 1943 the Ta 154 V 4 to V 7 prototypes were built by Focke-Wulf at Langenhagen, and in early 1944 these aircraft were given certificates of airworthiness. The first eight pre-series aircraft were built by the Gothaer Waggonfabrik in early 1944 at the Salzbergwerk Wremen.

The first production Ta 154 A-1 flew on 13 June 1944. The A-1 series was intended to be built at Wremen, while production of wings and undercarriages began at the Posen factory in Poland, and the fuselage with its pressurized cabin was simultaneously produced at Cottbus. At around this time bombing raids destroyed the firm of Goldman, which had produced the 'Tego Film' aircraft adhesive used for the TA 154's wooden components. Focke-Wulf therefore turned to Dynamit AG at Leverkusen for supplies of another adhesive, but this was still in the development stage and was only half as powerful. Professor Tank therefore decided to stop production. Since the Ta 154 programme would suffer considerable delays until an improved adhesive was available, the Air Ministry withdrew the order for series production and redeployed the underground production facility at Salzbergwerk Wremen. Only seven examples of the Ta 154 A-1 were built.

With Jumo 213 A engines the Ta 154 was still capable of 630km/h at an altitude of 8,500m; the Mosquito with its Rolls-Royce Merlin 21s could achieve 620km/h at 6,300m. The Ta 154 could attack Mosquitoes only at safe altitudes — not much of an advantage! Only with the use of the Jumo 213 E and GM-1 injection could this advantage be increased.

Left: Full-scale mock-up of the Ta 154, showing one of the six guns which formed its offensive armament, as well as the FuG 212 radar.

Left: Works Nos 320008 to 320010 were equipped as all-weather fighters (A-2/U4). Four aircraft were converted to night fighters designated Ta 154 A-4 shortly before the end of the war.

Left: Professor Kurt Tank stepping out of the first prototype Ta 154 at Hannover-Langenhagen on 7 July 1943.

Jet Aircraft

Right: Pilots of JG 1 assembled around their He 162 A-1/A-2s waiting for the British occupying forces on 6 May 1945.

Below: The He 280 V-2 ('GJ+CA') was destroyed on 26 June 1943 after an engine failure.

Heinkel He 280

In response to the Air Ministry Directive of 4 January 1939, Heinkel drew up the first design for a gas turbine-powered pursuit fighter with three MG 151/20 cannon as fixed armament. In the summer of 1939 two different models were produced of a fighter which was first designated He 180. On 26 September Air Ministry representatives inspected the mock-ups at the Rechlin Test Establishment, and from then on the aircraft was referred to as the He 280. As with other aircraft manufacturers, serious problems were encountered with the jet engines in terms of operational safety. It would be years before either the BMW P 3302 or the HeS 8A would be completely trouble-free. Meanwhile there were tests on the armament and ejection seat.

On 28 August 1940 the He 280 V1 was rolled out at Rostock-Marienehe and a month later it made an unpowered towed test flight, being towed into the air by a Heinkel He 111. By the end of 1940 the second prototype was in final assembly, and the He 280 V3 to V5 were partially complete. Heinkel was also trying to obtain a firm order from the Air Ministry for further test models up to V10. As there seemed to be no immediate prospect of either a fully functional BMW P 3302 or HeS 8A gas turbine, the possibility of using a pulse-jet was investigated. The first flight of the He 280 V2 with two HeS 8A engines took place on 30 March 1941. In June 1942 an Argus As 014 pulse-jet for the He 280 V1 was delivered to Rostock. By the end of October, the first prototype was equipped with four of these pulse-jets and at that point tests with the Heinkel jet engine were discontinued.

In July 1942 the He 280 V3 made its first flight using HeS 8A engines, although these were later replaced by two Jumo 004s. By the

Right: The He 280 V-3 ('GJ+CB') flew for the first time on 5 July 1942 and was powered by two HeS 8A jet engines.

Below right: The He 280 V-3 was put into store after the end of development at Vienna and remained there until May 1945.

Below: The He 280 V-1 first prototype made its first flight on 22 September 1940. The aircraft crashed, after 64 towed flights, on 13 January 1943.

winter of 1942 plans for 24 test models of the He 280 with Jumo and BMW jet engines had been drawn up. The He 280 V10 to V24 were designated as production series He 280 B-1s, which were to be provided with heavier nose armament (six guns). In addition, the possibility of adding a jettisonable rack beneath the fuselage centre-section was investigated. Because of high fuel consumption, the airframe had to be enlarged. Also the twin rudders had to be replaced by a single central rudder for production reasons. However, the He 280 fell behind the Me 262 on the basis of power calculations, and the Messerschmitt fighter was already further into its test programme. For these reasons, no further models of the He 280 were built after the V9 and in March 1943 the Air Ministry cancelled the production order. The remaining He 280s served mainly to test new rudder forms and most of the aircraft were later stored.

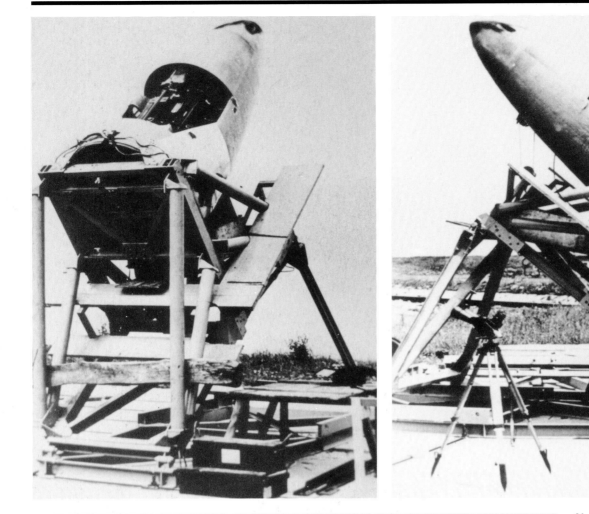

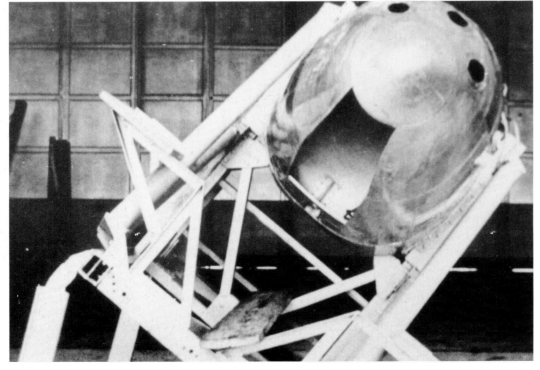

Above left and right: The test rig for the weapons platform of the He 280 B-1 during a static test at the factory.

Left: Three MG 151 cannon were intended as the armament for the planned He 280 B-1 series.

Summary of Heinkel He 280 Prototypes

Model	Code	First Flight	Engine	Remarks
V 1	'OL+AS'	22.09.1940	Unpowered	Crashed 13.01.1943 after 64 towed flights
		01.04.1941	HeS 8A	Airworthiness tests only
		13.01.1943	As 014	
V 2	'GJ+CA'	30.03.1941	HeS 8A	
		16.03.1943	Jumo 004	80 per cent damage following engine failure on 26.06.1943
V 3	'GJ+CB'	05.07.1942	HeS 8A	Components available in April 1945 at Schwechat
V 4	—	13.08.1943	BMW 003	Airworthiness only
		31.09.1944	Jumo 004	Airworthiness only, airframe at Hörsching in October 1944
V 5	—	26.07.1943	He S8A	Airworthiness only
		15.09.1943	BMW 003	Airworthiness only. Airframe stored in parts
V 6	—	26.07.1943	BMW 003	Airworthiness. Airframe stored in parts
V 7	'NU+EB' 'D-IXEM'	19.04.1943	Unpowered	115 towed flights to beginning of 1945
V 8	'NU+EC'	19.07.1943	Jumo 004	
		15.08.1943	He TL	Airworthiness only. In possession of DFS March 1945
V 9	—	31.08.1943	BMW 003	Airworthiness only. Airframe stored in parts
V 10	—	April 1943	Jumo 004	Planned airworthiness; first prototype He 280 B-1
V 11	—	May 1943	HMW 003A	Planned airworthiness; second prototype He 280 B-1s
V 12	—	June 1943	He TL	Planned airworthiness; third prototype He 280 B-1s

Messerschmitt Me 262

The design for the Messerschmitt Me 262 arose from the Me P 65/P 1065 project of 15 December 1938 for a 'High-Speed Fighter Aircraft for Operation Against Aerial Targets'. Flight tests began in April 1941 with a single Jumo 210 G piston engine installed in the nose. This was replaced by two BMW P 3302 turbojets as soon as their performance was deemed acceptable. On 25 March 1942 the V 1 took off using its jet engines, which however had a very short endurance so that the aircraft, which still retained its piston engine, had to land under propeller power. In the summer of 1942 the construction of five prototypes was authorized, for production in 1943. The V-prototypes had Jumo 004 engines, after it had been established that the power of the BMW gas turbine did not meet requirements.

During a meeting in August 1942, an increase in the number of V-prototypes to ten was requested by KdE. The power and

Right: The first production Me 262 (S-1, Works No 130006, 'VI+AF'), which made its maiden flight on 19 April 1944 and was used mainly for weapons testing.

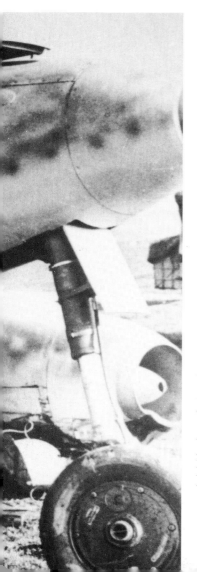

Below: This Me 262 A-1a (Works No 500079) was discovered by Allied troops at Giebelstadt on 4 April 1945. The machine had presumably belonged to KG(J) 54 and came originally from KG 51.

reliability of the jet engines were still not acceptable, so that flight tests with a few aircraft were possible at Messerschmitt only after some delays. Production conditions for these aircraft were established in March 1943, with equipment details following in Messerschmitt Factory Protocol No 11 of 28 May 1943. The construction of 100 Me 262 test models and zero-series aircraft was then approved by a KdE order of 10 April 1943 so as to complete testing on a broader basis. Out of this barely satisfactory situation arose the production order, which, on the cancellation of the Me 209, had been made on 25 May 1943 by Generalfeldmarschall Milch after consultations with Reichsmarschall Göring.

Up to May 1943, four Me 262s had been produced, all fitted with tail wheels. The test models not yet available (V 5 to V 10) were to be built through to March 1944, so the Me 262 V 5 became the first test model, in the summer of 1943, to be fitted with a nose wheel, though it was non-retractable. On 1 October 1942 the Me 262 V 2 made its first flight powered by Jumo 004 engines. It was followed into the air by Me 262 V 3 on 17 July, also with Jumo 004s. Testing of the V 4 began in April 1943.

Despite strenuous efforts, little useful data had been obtained up to December 1943 because so few aircraft were available. The KdE and GdJ therefore organized the establishment of Erprobungskommando Me 262 (Test Command) at Lechfeld airfield under the command of Hauptmann Thierfelder. The first aircraft supplied to the Erprobungskommando was the Me 262 V 5 with fixed undercarriage. It was used mainly

for training and apart from nose wheel tests yielded hardly any results. Performance and power trials began with the sixth and seventh prototypes which had been supplied meanwhile. With a large degree of participation by the firm Junkers at their Rechlin test establishment, engine tests of the Jumo 004 began. Considerable delays were experienced in the programme due to engine failures. At the same time, armament tests began, carried out selectively by Kommando Me 262 with the participation of the Rechlin and Tarnewitz test establish-ments.

The aircraft in the production programme of 16 June 1943 were regarded as a pre-production series. However, this did not come to fruition due to air raids on Messerschmitt's Augsburg and Regensburg factories. The series was further delayed by technical difficulties from the middle of January to the end of March 1944. To keep risks to the minimum, all technical departments were to be co-ordinated by the Model Supervisor. The intention was to bring together all necessary documents and test results as early as possible, in order to avoid further delays in the progress of the series. An important factor in this preliminary work was the establishment of a Stress Test Commission by Generalfeldmarschall Milch. This Commission consist-ed of delegates from the DVL, E-Stelle, and qualified engineers from the aircraft industry. Their work was especially important since the vibration and stress tests at Augsburg had been interrupted by enemy action. Production, which had started in March 1944, was again interrupted on 24 April by bombing raids on Leipheim. The first five

Final assembly of the zero-series of the Me 262 at Leipheim.

Left: Ground crew of the Me 262 at Lechfeld near Landsberg. In the background is a six-engined Me 323.

Right: All Me 262 A-1as were modified as auxiliary 'Blitz Bombers'.

production aircraft were produced by the E-Kommando in collaboration with Messerschmitt.

At Whitsun, during a meeting with the Reichsmarschall at Obersalzberg — and on a decision by the Führer himself — it was decided that the Me 262, which had been developed as a fighter and fighter-bomber, should become a 'Blitzbomber'. This command to produce a 'Maximum-Speed Bomber' produced, during the threatened invasion of France, an accelerated test programme which was inevitably limited to necessities and front-line applications.

The emergency tests carried out at the Rechlin Research Establishment covered the technical usefulness for the role of 'Maximum-Speed Bomber'. Most tests were carried out at Rechlin-Lärz. The EKL took over servicing of the aircraft and the task of organizing flying operations. The tests included power trials (E 2), range tests with two 250kg and one 500kg bombs (E 2), take-off tests with bombs and two RI 502s (E 2), engine tests with six aircraft at EKL Lärz and with two aircraft at E 3 (E 3), radar and target spotting tests (E 4), tests on hydraulic and electrical equipment as well as on course steering (component testing for fighter control and bombing) (E 5), bomb and loading trials for two 250kg (BT 200c) or one 500kg and BT 400, tests of the BZA bombsight installation and bombing pattern (E 7), as well as the use of various towing machinery and towing harnesses for nose-wheel aircraft and supercharged-engine transport vehicles (E 8). The BZA sight proved unsatisfactory so the TSA 2 was to be installed and tested. The course steering equipment was necessary, and additional tanks were to be installed to increase range.

The tests at Rechlin began on 10 June 1944 when the first aircraft became available. Delivery of twelve further Me 262s continued until July 1944. Undercarriage problems delayed the test programme by a further four weeks. However, by 20 September 1944, 350 flying hours and over 800 take-offs had been recorded at Rechlin. The service capability of the aircraft as a fighter was reported by telegram to the KdE on 12 September 1944. At the same time results of fighter tests, including nine 'kills', were also advised.

The evaluation of flying characteristics and performance after the tests gave satisfactory roll rate, and also good stability about the main axis. The high control forces above 600km/h, however, made it necessary to install a trim control for fighter application. This was introduced on the 146th machine. In general, the aircraft was easy to fly and exhibited no tendency to yaw to either side. Take-offs and landings as a fighter could be carried out by an average pilot. The only extra pilot training needed was with respect to the jet engine.

All-round pilot visibility was excellent; the windscreen had already proved itself. Positive instrument and blind-flying properties were established over many night and bad-weather trials. Improvements were also made in the landing gear, and as a result landing weight could be increased from 5,300 to

5,700kg. Take-off weight in the 'Blitzbomber' role was normally around 7,100kg. For use as a 'Blitzbomber', two of the four cannon were removed and the gun apertures sealed.

Functional tests of bombing capability were carried out by arrangement between the E-Stelle and Messerschmitt for amendments to the Messerschmitt ('Viking Ship') rack. In the series construction, the ETC 504 rack was used as it was capable of carrying the required drop load. On the 'Viking Ship', the SC 250, SD 250, AB 250-2, SC 500, SD 500 and AB 500-1 could be carried, but not the AB 500-3, BT 200 or ER 4 Schloss 50. On the ETC 504 or 503, the SC 250, SD 250, AB 250-2, SD 500, SC 500, AB 500-1, AB 500-3 and BT 200 could be carried. Only the BT 400 could not be carried as it protruded over the undercarriage fairings. Bombs of 50kg could only be carried with the AB 500-3.

Below: This Me 262 was attached to Erprobungskommando (Jagd) [Fighter Test Command], which was transferred to the Nowotny Kommando, which later became III.(Erg)/JG 2.

Bottom: An Me 262 A-1a of JV 44 (Galland) in service at Munich.

Summary of Me 262

Me 262 A-1a Jet fighter with two Jumo 004B engines

Me 262 A-1b Jet fighter with two BMW 003B engines

Me 262 A-1a/R-1 Equipped with R4M rockets as armament

Me 262 A-1/Bo Auxiliary 'Blitzbomber'

Me 262 A-1a/U1 Mixed armament with two MK 103, MK 108 and MG 151 (planned series construction)

Me 262 A-1a/U2 All-weather fighter with FuG 125

Me 262 A-1a/U3 Unarmed reconnaissance version (modification of Me 262 A-1a)

Me 262 A-1a/U4 Heavy jet fighter with 50mm MK 214

Me 262 A-1a/U5 Heavy jet fighter with six nose-mounted MK 108s

Below: JV 44 had 55 confirmed kills to its credit.

Bottom: One of some 180 Me 262 A-1as ('B3+GR') delivered in March 1945 to Kampfgeschwader (Jagd) 54 at Neuburg/Donau.

Me 262 A-2a 'Blitzbomber' with reduced armament (two MK 108s)

Me 262 A-2a/R 'Blitzbomber' with reinforced armour

Me 262 A-2a/U1 'Blitzbomber' with TSA sight

Me 262 A-2a/U2 Two-seat high-speed bomber (Lotfe-Bomber)

Me 262 A-3a Armoured aircraft I and II

Me 262 A-4a Previous designation for Me 262 A-1a/U1 and A-1a/U3

Me 262 A-5a Armed reconnaissance aircraft

Me 262 B-1a Two-seat trainer

Me 262 B-1a/U1Z Two-seat auxiliary night fighter

Me 262 B-2a Two-seat night fighter with Jumo 004s

Me 262 C-1a Interceptor with two Jumo 004Bs and one rear-mounted HWK rocket engine (Heimatschutzer I)

Me 262 C-2b Interceptor with two BMW 003Rs (Heimatschutzer II)

Me 262 C-3a Interceptor with two Jumo 004Bs and one jettisonable HWK rocket engine mounted beneath the fuselage

De 262 D-1 Provisional designation for Me 262 C-2b

Me 262 E-1 Preliminary designation for Me 262 A-1a/U4

Me 262 S Zero-series model for Me 262 A-1a

Me 262 V Test model for Me 262

Me 262 W Provisional designation for Me 262 with pulse-jet engines

Conversion packs for the Me 262

R 1 Jettisonable rack under the fuselage for 500-litre fuel tank

R 2 JATO rocket (presumably RI-502) for overload take-off

R 3 Built-in, non-jettisonable rocket engine as additional thrust for the 'Heimatschutzer' (Project)

R 4 FuG 350 Zc 'Naxos' radar for night and bad-weather use (passive radar, corresponding to the British H2S radar), and FuG 218 'Neptun V' active target-seeking radar

R 5 Fixed armament MK 108

R 6 Fighter-bomber equipped with 503 A-1 bomb rack and TSA-D2 sight

R 7 Unguided R4M 'Orkan' air-to-air missile

R 8 Rheinmetall-Borsig R 100 BS unguided air-to-air rocket missile

R 9 Ruhrstahl 8-344 (X-4) wire-guided missile

Below: An Me 262 A-1a of 7./KG (J) 54 during an engine test. In the cockpit is Oberfeldwebel Gentzsh.

Right: The 'Yellow 7' of III./JG 7 at Fürth in the early summer of 1945.

Below right: Fhr Hans-Guido Mütke of 9./JG 7 flew this aircraft (Works No 500071) to Switzerland on 24 April 1945.

Above left: Dismantling an Me 262 A-1a/R1. The R4M gratings under the wings are clearly visible.

Left: Changing an engine at Lechfeld. In the background is the Me 262 V-8.

Above: An aerial view of Lechfeld (taken by the US 8th Air Force) where the Me 262 was tested and where III.(Erg)/JG 2 was stationed from 1944.

Right: Lechfeld airfield in May 1945. On the left is the Me 262 V-12 (Works No 170074) without engines. This had formerly been designated the Me 262 C-2b powered by two BMW 003 R jet engines.

Left: One of the few Me 262 B-1a two-seaters. It was converted from an Me 262 A-1a by Blohm und Voss at Wesendorf.

Below left: Several destroyed Me 262 A-1a aircraft of KG(J) 54 were discovered at Neuburg/Donau in the summer of 1945.

Above: Production of Me 262s was transferred to the forest because of Allied air superiority

Below: American troops examine a damaged Me 262 A-1a of KG 51 at Frankfurt on 27 March 1945.

Heinkel He 162

Although in the Messerschmitt Me 262 the Luftwaffe had a powerful and highly developed jet aircraft, emphasis was still given to the development of other gas turbine-powered fighters. The Me 262 conformed to the quality criterion of the years 1940-1943, in that it was not then strictly necessary to keep production as simple as possible. At that time emphasis was on developing and producing everything to a 'schön und gut' (zero defects) standard.

After the change in priorities that placed fighters ahead of bombers, the increase in fighter production depended less upon the competitiveness of the airframe manufacturer and much more on the availability of constructional materials and fuel. Since these essentials were scarcer for the Germans than they were for the Allies, all possible economies and reductions had to be made.

In view of the aerial war situation, the training conditions for pilots, and the poor reliability of the jet engines then available, a long service life was not expected of jet aircraft. It was estimated that an Me 262 would be a total loss after five to ten missions. The Me 262, furthermore, required two jet engines and correspondingly more fuel, which in view of the rapidly worsening war situation was becoming increasingly scarce. The idea of building a single-engined jet fighter of about half the size, and therefore with similar performance, had much to commend it.

In the summer of 1944 Heinkel were already working on their Project P 1073, a high-speed jet fighter powered by one or two He 011 gas turbines. On 19 July that year, plans were also made for a jet fighter powered by a single BMW 003 engine. These developments were due mainly to the good

Left: The first prototype of the Messerschmitt P 1101. The aircraft is fitted with a model of the HeS 11 A-1 turbine.

Right: Model test of the Me P 1112/S-2, carried out in connection with the design of the Me P 1101/1110 and the 1111/1112. Development was in progress at the beginning of April 1945.

information supplied by Carl Frydag, Heinkel's General Director and close colleague of the Rüstungstab. On 8 September the Amt der Technischen Luftrüstung (Office of Air Technical Equipment, or TLR) produced the specification for a 'Volksjäger' (People's Fighter). Invitations to tender were given to the firms of Arado (E 580), Blohm und Voss (P 211), Dornier, Fieseler, Focke-Wulf ('Volksflitzer'), Heinkel (modified P 1073), Messerschmitt and Junkers (EF 123 and 124). The requirement was for a: gas turbine-powered fighter aircraft with the BMW 003 engine; employing the most economical construction method of wood and steel; maximum speed of 750km/h at sea-level; take-off distance to be not more than 500m; stable undercarriage for rough terrain; 30min endurance at 100 per cent thrust power at sea-level; instrumented for all-weather use, with FuG 16 ZY or FuG 15 radar; armoured against 13mm shells for both pilot and ammunition; two MK 108 (100 rounds) or MG 151/20 (250 rounds) armament; fuel tank armour or provision for drop-tank; mass production with the simplest equipment; easy to fly; using as many components as possible of the Bf 109 or Fw 190 (this requirement was fulfilled by none of the firms!); suitable for transport by road; and with a total weight of not more than 2 tonnes.

Because they had already been working on the project, it took only three days for Heinkel to produce a design based on Project P 1073 for the Head of the TLR, and as early as 20 September 1944 the first prototype of the Volksjäger was produced. Nine days later the RMfRuK gave the order for production of the Volksjäger without waiting for test results. The first flight was to follow at the beginning of

Right: The only P 1101 to be completed was captured in damaged condition on 29 April 1945 when Oberammergau was occupied.

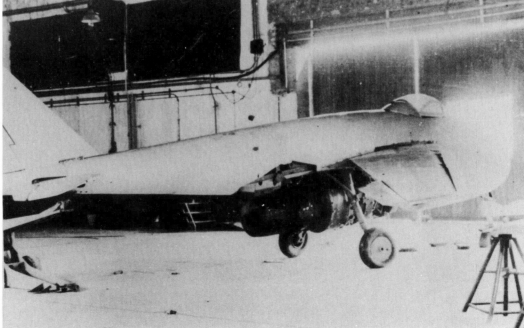

December 1944 and main production was to begin in the following March.

At the end of October, series production began and on 1 December the He 162 was ready for take-off. Taxiing tests began the next day, and on 6 December the He 162 V1 made its first flight at Schwechat-Heidfeld, near Vienna. This was made possible by the 1,360 Heinkel workers in Vienna working 90-hour weeks, later reduced to 70, as well as a system known as 'raschen Entscheidung' ('swift decision' — on-the-spot solutions to small problems).

The aircraft was a shoulder-wing design with a retractable nose-wheel undercarriage and was powered by a BMW 003 E engine with quick-release mountings so that it could be changed easily. The fuselage and rudder were of aluminium, the wings and tailplane of wood, with other components in steel. The Junkers-built He 162 A-1 was to have two 50-round MK 108s while the A2 series produced by Heinkel had two 120-round MG 151/20s. As the MK 108 had greater hitting power (one hit was considered to be enough to shoot down a Mustang, and three enough to shoot down a B-17), the A-1 was intended for action against bombers, with the A-2 reserved for anti-fighter attacks. Since by occupying Posen the Soviet

Army brought production of the MK 108 to a halt, the Volksjäger was produced only as the He 162 A-2.

The first prototype crashed on 10 December 1944, and further test flights with the He 162 V 2 led to strengthening of the wing skin. To reduce the aircraft's tendency to pitch-down, anhedral wing tips were installed, among other measures. To improve stability, Heinkel reduced the fuselage fuel tank and added weight to the nose, thus moving the centre of gravity forwards. The more elegant solution, an extension of the fuselage, was dismissed because of production difficulties. A further problem arose from the position of the engine, which was mounted above the fuselage. This meant that during turning manoeuvres the twin rudders could be affected by the jet exhaust, from which they could not then be moved, putting aircraft out of control.

On 14 January 1945 the first He 162 from Heinkel (EHAG-Nord) was produced at Rostock. At the end of the month DLH at Oranienburg undertook final assembly. Production at Rostock was held up because of lack of rudder components, and at Vienna barely twelve He 162s had been produced.

In February 1945 General der Jagdflieger Gollob planned to give clearance for the first

Above: The first prototype of the Heinkel He 162 V-1 (Works No 200001, 'VI+IA'), which first flew on 6 December 1944 piloted by Gotthold Peter.

Above: The first 'Volksjäger' (People's Fighter) produced by Junkers (JFM) on 23 March 1945.

Right: The first He 162 A-1 rolls off the production line at Heinkel's Oranienburg factory on 24 March 1945.

delivered to JG 1. Simultaneously models were made available to two squadrons (2. and 3./JG 1) for training purposes. These were located at Parchim and Heidfeld near Vienna. On 5 March 1945 the first test aircraft was delivered to the Test Establishment at Rechlin. By mid-March about 70 aircraft were under construction at the Junkers Bernburg factory, although they were held up by the lack of undercarriages. On 1 April 1945, I./JG 1 still had only four He 162s. A week later production of the He 162 was discontinued in favour of the Me 262 A-1.

On 11 April 1945, 2./JG 1 was transferred as Stabstaffel JG 1 from Lechfeld and Memmingen to serve as EKdo Lechfeld 162. For the first Gruppe, sixteen He 162s were now available. By the end of April the I.Einsatzgruppe/JG 1 was given clearance to use the Volksjäger, and several air battles followed between then and 5 May 1945. The only confirmed 'kill' was credited to Lt. R. Schmitt who on 4 May shot down a Typhoon. The British pilot was taken prisoner, and became a guest in the Staff Officers' Mess. No one dealt with him badly when he showed his pleasure at the news that British tanks were already at Leck. On 6 May the base was occupied by British troops. A few days previously, on 1 May, the squadron had 40 He 162s on charge, of which 30 were serviceable.

combat flight of the aircraft in mid-April 1945, and the first active group in mid-May. Both targets were exceeded by two weeks. On 26 February the first Junkers-built He 162 was

Above left: The day after the Oranienburg aircraft was rolled out the Marienehe factory produced its first He 162 Volksjäger.

Left: The 'Languste' underground factory at Mödling near Vienna as it is today.

Above: Eleven undamaged Volksjägers (AM 58 to 68) were taken to England after the war or distributed among the Allies.

Right: This He 162 shows all the Gruppe emblems of Jagdgeschwader 1.

Above: Einsatzgruppe I./JG 1 was formed from I. and II./JG 1 in 1945 at Leck.

Left: An He 162 A-2 discovered in a south German scrapyard.

Rocket Aircraft

Above: Four Bachem Natters were captured at St Leonhard in Austria in May 1945.

Right: An aircraft in service with JG 400 at Brandis. On 14 April 1945, two days before their capture by enemy troops, almost all Me 163s were blown up.

Messerschmitt Me 163

The Me 163 B rocket-powered fighter was a cantilever tailless mid-wing monoplane of mixed construction with jettisonable undercarriage and retractable landing skids and tailwheel. The fuselage was a circular cross-section monocoque of overlapping, flush-riveted duralumin panels. They were attached to an armoured nose-cone which also served as ballast in keeping the centre of gravity forward. The single-seat cockpit had an armoured glass canopy and armour plating. The aircraft was powered by a Walter R II 211 (HWK 109-509) liquid-fuelled rocket engine. The two fuels were respectively 'C-Stoff' (methanol, hydrazine hydrate, and water with traces of sodium cuprocyanide as a catalyst) and 'T-Stoff' (hydrogen peroxide). The C-Stoff fuel tanks were located in the wings; the unarmoured fuel tank for T-Stoff

was immediately behind the pilot. The wing had fixed slats and landing flaps, with the trim controls mounted outboard and inboard on the wing trailing edge. The ailerons also served as elevators. Radio equipment consisted of FuG 16 ZE and FuG 25.

As early as 1941 design work for a new rocket-powered fighter with a more powerful engine than the Me 163 A, higher fuel capacity, and a modified wing and fuselage was already at an advanced stage. The project description was issued by the Air Ministry on 22 September 1941. At the same time the Walter factory at Kiel and BMW at Berlin-Spandau were both given the order to produce a more powerful rocket engine.

Construction of the Me 163 B began in the autumn of 1941. The prototype was to be built by Messerschmitt at Augsburg and 68

Left: The first Messerschmitt Me 163 carried the designation AV4 ('KE+SW') and had its first towed test flight on 13 February 1941.

Above: After an exhibition at Peenemünde on 25 August 1942, the Me 163 AV5 was burnt out.

further aircraft at Regensburg. From the Me 163 B V 23, engine installation was done by Klemm at Böblingen, who were also responsible for making all modifications and improvements which occurred during production. On 26 June 1942 the Me 163 B V 1 began unpowered towed test flights. By mid-1943, due to the lack of a functional HWK 509-109 engine, the R II 203 rocket engine of the Me 163 A was used. Later the engine originally intended became available in larger quantities and in reasonably reliable condition. By early 1944 series production of the Me 163 B was well under way. When production ended in January 1945, a total of 364 Me 163 B had been built.

In February 1944 the OKL gave the order to equip the first Jagdgruppe with Me 163 rocket aircraft; this was Jagdgruppe 400. It was recruited from Erprobungskommando 16, which had been stationed at Bad Zwischenahn and had the responsibility for testing the Me 163. Some weeks later the Jagdgruppe was moved to Wittmundhafen, where a second Staffel was formed. In May 1944 the unit had thirteen rocket fighters, of which only one aircraft was serviceable; the remaining machines were used only for armament testing.

After several air battles against Allied bombers, the build-up of JGr 400 went ahead rapidly. On 31 July 1944 the staff and three squadrons of the group were established. The last of these were based at Stargard. Ergänzungsstaffel 400 with nine Me 163 Bs and some Bf 110s used as tugs was based at Udetfeld. In addition, the establishment of a fourth group with six squadrons and a towing squadron began at Kölleda.

In the late summer of 1944 the first and second squadrons of Jagdgruppe 400 were located at Brandis. There, both squadrons were merged, and Jagdgruppe 400 was expanded to become Jagdgeschwader 400. On 12 November 1944 came the order for a second Gruppe of JG 400, made up of the 3rd and 4th squadrons. Also, the Ergänzungsstaffel, which

meanwhile had been based at Lechfeld, was transformed into an Ergänzungsgruppe. There was also the V.(Ergänzungs)/JG 2 with the 13th to 15th squadrons, which was made up of parts of EK 16; based at Sprottau, it was used for pilot training. In December 1944, JG 400, equipped with 109 Me 163 Bs, was located not only at Brandis but also at bases in Leuna, Pölitz, and Heydebreck.

In April 1945, I./JG 400 had 32 Me 163 Bs and the second Gruppe had about thirteen aircraft. On 7 March the Staff of JG 400, and on 19 April its first and second Gruppen, were dissolved by the OKL. By now replacement by the Me 263 was not possible.

Summary of Me 163 B

Me 163 B-0 V 1 to V 70
latest equipment and modifications from all production series
Engine: HWK 109-509 A
Armament: 2 MG 151/20s to Me 163 BV 45
2 MK 108s from Me 163 BV 46
Radio: FuG 25a and Fug 16 ZE
Me 163 B-0/R1 20 aircraft as Me 163 B-0
Engine: HWK 109-509 A
Armament: 2 MK 108s
Radio: FuG 25a and FuG 16 ZE
Me 163 B-0/R2 30 aircraft as Me 163 B-0, but with the mass-produced wing of the Me 163 B-1
Engine: HWK 109-509 A
Armament: 2 MK 108s

Radio: FuG 25a and FuG 16 ZE
Me 163 B-1/R1 70 aircraft, forward fuselage of the Me 163 B-0, tail section of Me 163 B-1, but with tailplane and rudder, mass-produced wing of the Me 163 B-1
Engine: HWK 109-509 A (with cruise chamber)
Armament: 2 MK 108s
Radio: FuG 25a and FuG 16 ZY
Me 163 B-1 approx. 390 aircraft mass-produced with built-in cruise chamber
Engine: HWK 109-509 A (with cruise chamber)
Armament: 2 MK 108s
Radio: FuG 25a and FuG 16 ZY
Me 163 B-2 Design of whole airframe according to mass-produced requirements of the Me 163 B-0 (without cruise chamber)
Engine: HWK 109-509 A (without cruise chamber)
Armament: 2 MK 108s
Radio: FuG 25a and FuG 16 ZY
Me 163 C-1 Further development of Me 163 B with cranked wings
Engine: HWK 109-509 A (with cruise chamber)
Armament: 2 MK 103s (wing transition)
2 MK 108s (fuselage)
Radio: FuG 25a and FuG 16 ZY

Note that the data given here includes planned production at 23 March 1944 and therefore differs from the number of aircraft produced.

Above: The Me 163 BV21 (Works No 163 10030, 'VA+SS') flew for the first time with a live engine on 24 June 1943. The test machine was used mainly for landing gear and engine power trials.

Right: The cockpit of an Me 163 B-1.

Right: The Me 163 B-1's sprung landing skid.

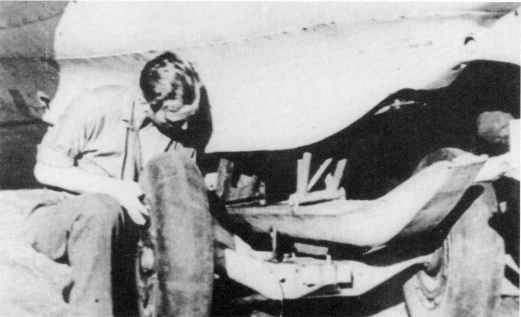

Left: The hydraulically retractable tail-wheel of the Me 163 B-1.

Left: Test run of an Me 163 B-1 by I./JG 400.

Left: For the Me 163 a special vehicle, the 'Scheuch-Schlepper', was developed.

Right: A model of the Ju 248 (Me 236 A-1) in the wind tunnel at the Junkers works at Dessau, remains of which may still be seen today.

Right: Cockpit mock-up of the planned Ju 248 A-1.

Bachem
Ba 349

The Bachem Ba 349 was evolved from an original concept which was submitted to the Air Ministry. During the summer of 1944 Erich Bachem and Willy Fiedler cooperated on a project for a single-seat fighter with a very high rate of climb. One of the basic requirements was a jettisonable trolley undercarriage. Hans Jordanoff, a colleague of Bachem, eventually decided to bring the idea to the attention of the Air Ministry. In addition to the Head of OKL TLR, the design was simultaneously brought to the attention of the SS Fuhrungshauptamt in 1944.

The Bachem was intended to be powered by a HWK 109-509 A-2 liquid-fuelled rocket engine, plus four solid-fuel rockets for take-off from a ramp. Because of the danger of explosion involved in the use of special fuel, Bachem envisaged that the pilot and airframe would land separately by parachute. This meant that the pilot would only have to be trained to fly and shoot; thus the lengthy training in landing and take-off could be dispensed with. After the end of the mission only the armament and the cabin would be lost.

The armament of the 5.72m-long interceptor consisted of two MK 108 cannon and 24 spin-stabilized 'Föhn' rockets, later increased to 48. After reaching its maximum altitude of 12,000m, the 1,700kg Ba 349 reached an average speed of 800km/h. The operational radius was a mere 20km, which required very accurate fighter direction. For this reason the BP 20 (as the type was originally designated) was rightly known as a 'manned anti-aircraft rocket'.

In September 1944 the Air Ministry ordered fifteen prototypes and designated the project Ba 349 in the fighter production programme. After that, full production followed in all building groups. In December 1944 the Ba 349 M-1 was completed with a launch trolley and the M-2 and M-3 with a

Left: An unmanned Bachem BP 20 'Natter' on the launching pad at Heuberg.

Above: Vertical launch of the BP 20 M17 from the 12.5m high launch pad.

Above right: Model of a Ba 349 with a R4M honeycomb, which could take 24 of these projectiles.

Right: Tests of the solid fuel auxiliary launch rockets at the Bachem works at Waldsee.

fixed undercarriage which had been modified from a Klemm Kl 35. This allowed the possibility of towed trials to determine flying characteristics. That month the first HWK 105-509 A-1 engine was installed at Waldsee and the first towed flight was made with the Ba 349 M-3 at Neuburg-Donau. At the end of December 1944 the first successful unmanned vertical launch was made at Heuberg bei Stetten, after an initial failure. Simultaneously, up to the end of January 1945, wind-tunnel testing on a small scale model was being carried out at the DVL.

On 14 February 1945 the Ba 349 M-8 made a towed test flight which also included the first free flight without power. A week later the first fully realistic vertical take-off test of a powered machine, including a test separation, took place. The pilot dummy and the tail section came down safely to earth by parachute. On 1 March the Ba 349 M-23 faced its first take-off. It was intended to be the first manned vertical take-off. The pilot, Lothar Siebel, lost his life.

Up to the end of March several unmanned vertical take-offs followed. On the 20th of that month, however, General Dornberger removed the Ba 349 from the test programme. Also the

SS showed no further interest, since no fuel for use for this kind of aircraft was available. Nevertheless, the Ba 349 continued to be built at Waldsee and Nabern/Teck. Some 35 aircraft were produced. From April 1945 the transfer of the Bachem factory to Bad Wörrishofen took place, where an advance command remained for only a short time. Together with five production models, important construction details, solid fuel rockets, and replacement components, some Bachem workers were captured by Americans at St Leonhard in Austria at the beginning of May.

Top, left and right: A total of 34 Natters were built or were in preparation before the end of the war.

Above centre: Launch preparations at Heuberg. The first unmanned launch (M7) took place on 18 December 1944, with the first manned launch (M23) on 1 March 1945.

Above: Wooden mock-up of a series type of Ba 349 A-1 with R4M armament.

Recommended Reading

J.R.Smith and Anthony L.Kay; *German Aircraft of the Second World War*, Putnam, 1972

Bryan Philpott; *History of the German Air Force*, Hamlyn, 1986

Bill Gunston; *The Illustrated Encyclopedia of Aircraft Armament*, Salamander, 1987

Encyclopedia of Aviation, Reference International, 1977

Matthew Cooper; *The German Air Force 1933-45: An Anatomy of Failure*, Jane's, 1981

William Green; *Warplanes of the Third Reich*, MacDonald, 1970

Above: Full-scale mock-up of the Arado Ar 240 V-11. Clearly visible are the pressurized cockpit and MG 151/20 mounted at the side of the fuselage.

Below: For the Ar 240 heavyfighter a remote-controlled MG 131 and an MG 151 were fitted as defensive armament.

Above: The Arado Ar 234 B-2 bomber, construction of which began in September 1944 at Landeshut/Schlesien, was the forerunner of the Ar 234 B-2/N auxiliary night fighter.

Below: Model of the Ar 234 C-5. From November 1944, a night fighter version (Ar 234 C-5/N) was wind-tunnel tested.

Acknowledgements

Sincere thanks for help and the supply of documents and photographs are due to: G. Aders, Th. Arens (Forschungsgruppe Luftfahrtgeschichte e.V.), U. Balke, V. Beyler, M. Boehme, E. Creek, H. Fritz, P. Heck, D. Herwig (Deutsche Studienbüro für Luftfahrt), K-E. Heinkel, Dr. Hiller, H.J. Nowarra, van Mol, F. Müller-Romminger, F. Offer, P. Petrick, J. Prowan, W. Radinger, Dipl.Ing. Ramson (ERNO/MBB), G. Schlaug, H. Schliephake, Ph. Schreiber, F. Selinger, Dipl.Ing. Schubert (MTU), R. Smith, H.H. Stapfer, Dr. Wustrack, (Flughafen Frankfurt AG) and Dipl.Ing. Zucker (Deutsches Museum München).

We must also thank Frau Monika Müller for careful preparation of the manuscript as well as my daughter, Nathalie Katharina Dressel, who read the text.

Manfred Griehl, Joachim Dressel
Mainz/Hochheim, Summer 1992

Left: Herbert Dieks, Wolfgang Heinemann, Klaus Metzner and Hermann Neninger in front of the Lippisch DM 1 glider discovered at Prien am Chiemsee. The DM 1 was intended to test the unusual delta configuration for the planned jet and rocket-powered fighters.

Left: The DM 1 at Prien awaiting transport to the USA in the summer of 1945.